SANITY CRUSHING CHILDHOODS and authentic Hope seem incongruent, but Robert Day and I both know they can be found when kids like us let Jesus Christ and caring adults in. Philippians 3:13 is Robert's testimony, my testimony and God's call to all who are listening and willing to respond.

— R.B. MITCHELL, AUTHOR OF CASTAWAY KID,
A FOCUS ON THE FAMILY PUBLICATION

NO CHILD SHOULD HAVE the memories Robert Day has—but God took the shattered pieces of his life and turned them into a beautiful mosaic of His grace. Now Robert uses the pain of his past to help heal children who need a home and someone to love them. In his compelling book, *Worst of Mothers: Best of Moms*, we receive an important reminder that Christian principles and compassion can go a long way with a child.

— MICHELLE COX, AUTHOR OF JUST 18 SUMMERS

ROBERT DAY USES HIS PERSONAL STORY to illuminate the tragic circumstances of too many of our children today. He calls for the Body of Christ—the Church, to take its place in responding to the needs of children and families. He is honest in telling his story, knowing that it does not speak to all circumstances, but that too many children have backgrounds similar to his and they need to hear a word of hope. The Church needs to hear this encouraging word and the role it can play in bringing hope to children and families.

— CLIFFORD ROSENBOHM, PH.D., ACSW, LCSW DIRECTOR,
SCHOOL OF SOCIAL WORK GEORGE FOX UNIVERSITY

Worst of *Mothers...* Best of *Moms*

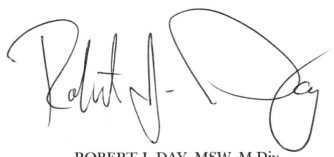

ROBERT J. DAY, MSW, M.Div
CEO of Patrick Henry Family Services

Published by
Patrick Henry Family Services Publishing
1621 Enterprise Drive
Lynchburg, VA 24502
434-239-6891
patrickhenry.org

Cover design by Richard McClintock
Interior design by Jon Marken, Lamp-Post Publicity
Editing by Jennifer Wall, David Marshall,
Myra Green, Richard McClintock, and Jon Marken
Marketing by Beckie Nix

Printed in the United States of America

ISBN: 978-0-9979026-0-0

DEDICATED

To JoAnne, Doris (Moe), Joyce, and Karen:
Four women who love.

Any Christian who is not a hero is a pig.
Leon Bloy

Contents

Preface 11

Acknowledgements 15

Introduction — The Social Problem River 17

Chapter 1 — Rejected 23

Chapter 2 — Taken 35

Chapter 3 — Abused 49

Chapter 4 — Abandoned 61

Chapter 5 — Bullied 75

Chapter 6 — Exploited 89

Chapter 7 — Rescued 105

Epilogue — The Church Response 121

Appendix A — Common Sense or Death:
The Patrick Henry Way 135

Appendix B — These Things We Believe 141

Family Pictures 147

About the Author 163

Preface

MOST PEOPLE WHO KNOW ME PERSONALLY would say that I am a good husband and father. I think most would even say that I am a good man. But I shouldn't be. The odds were not in my favor that I would turn out as well as I did.

For many years my wife and kids have been asking, almost begging, me to write this book. Whenever I give my testimony in church, or share a portion of my story with a captive audience, invariably someone will suggest that I write a book. For the longest time I would smile, nod my head in affirmation, and say to myself, *"Yeah, right."*

I have not suffered from lack of encouragement or even motivation. I always thought it was a good idea. What kept me from putting my story down on paper is that it lacked, as the creation did in the beginning, form and organized substance. I could tell it in snippets, but there was never any cohesive structure. I simply could not figure out how to go about it. My story is such a convoluted mess, even I don't completely understand it. To this day I still don't remember all the events in proper sequence, and because of that a linear account didn't seem plausible.

Then one day I was inspired by the gospel accounts of the life of Jesus. The four gospel authors often grouped the events and teachings of their Master by themes and presented them in ways that emphasized the larger message they were trying to convey to their readers. The point of the whole gospel is greater than any of its particular parts. That was the breakthrough I needed to begin building the anatomy of my story. I now had form as well as purpose. Once I began to fully appreciate that the events of my life culminate in an overall message—that there is a moral to the story—the words began flowing rather naturally.

The chapters are not necessarily in chronological order but instead are arranged largely by subject matter. Each chapter not only records the challenges I faced but presents the concerns and troubles experienced by millions of helpless children every day. These various child-welfare matters now absorb billions of our tax dollars and waste countless precious lives, yet we don't seem any closer to solving them. My story brings perspective and possible solutions to these larger vexing issues.

The subject of poverty, for example, is a consistent theme in my childhood. I emphasize it strongly in chapter three. However, the point of that chapter isn't that I lived in poverty. That's not distinct to my story. The point is that poverty lived in me, and by breaking the stronghold of poverty we can set millions of children free to enjoy healthier and more productive lives. Intertwined in the narrative of the story itself is commentary that attempts to answer the question I get all the time, "How did you get out of that mess?" The conclusion then follows that other children can get out, too, by similar means.

As I wrote I continued to wrestle with the overall purpose of the book. Why would anyone want to read about my tragic childhood? Although there was a time I would have craved it, I'm not looking for pity. That's a dead-end street. Others have suffered much more than I have. It seems small-minded and self-serving to talk about my childhood in light of the tragic lives of so many of the world's children. I have never been a victim of terrorism or suffered pervasive starvation or the evil of human trafficking. In comparison, I've had a nice life.

Additionally, I haven't accomplished anything noteworthy enough to inspire interest in my biography. I haven't invented or built anything of consequence. I've never been elected to a political office. I have no fame to emulate or fortune to covet. The only thing I seem to have accomplished is breaking the chain of poverty and stopping the cycle of familial dysfunction. What would be the point, then, of my memoir?

The answer finally came to me. After grouping the chapters of my story together in themes instead of points in time, I began to see a possible purpose. The apostle Paul wrote in Romans 8:28, "And we know that in all things God works for the good of those who love him, who have been called according to his purposes."

My life story is part of my life purpose. The story serves as a map to my own hidden treasure, my divine purpose. The two are irrevocably intertwined. My calling is connected to my childhood; my childhood is fastened firmly to my life of service. The Lord has repurposed my pain for His own good reason. He has beautifully recycled my trauma and turned it into something positive. If sharing my story helps others, then it has served a wonderful purpose. Yet it isn't about me or even my story. It has to be about more than that or I would not have written it.

The account of my childhood is presented here only in the earnest desire that those I am called to serve might have better outcomes. The point of this book is to inspire involvement of others, to rally those who are like-minded, and to move the work of rescuing children forward. The foundation of this project is to spark a movement that somehow changes the life stories of thousands, maybe even tens-of-thousands, of vulnerable children and distressed families. Hopefully, it will also encourage those already in the fight to renew their efforts.

It is my sincerest hope to see the church awakened to its special calling to "suffer not the children" and to once again practice a "pure and undefiled religion." That would be sufficient justification for the few pages presented here.

As you study what I have written, please understand you are reading three authors, not one. The first author is a child of poverty and abuse. I tell the story from my childhood memories, or my memory of what others told me about my experiences. Those memories may be flawed or the viewpoint missing certain contexts that children don't usually know or understand at the time. The second author is an adult social worker. The commentary you will read throughout is heavily influenced by my professional education and experience as a tainted grown-up. Undoubtedly, the second author is analyzing everything that happened to the first and making certain judgment calls about it. A Christian minister serves as the third author. Here I attempt to stand above the first two authors in order to provide a certain faith perspective. It should be recognized that the third author may be the most biased but also the most helpful of the three.

With that goal in mind, I pray the Lord's purposes be accomplished by the message of this publication, that you might be blessed in the reading of it and that the children of heartbreaking circumstances might be ministered to by an army of compassionate servants.

Acknowledgements

WHEN DECIDING THAT THE TIME had come to write, I was showered with support, patience, and inspiration. First, I would like to thank the boys and girls that we serve at PHFS, as well as the staff. Their character-based determination is a deep well of energy from which I draw buckets each day. I would also like to acknowledge the Board of Trustees, Executive Officers, and the Advancement team of PHFS. All have given me support since the very beginning of the writing process.

I applaud Jon Marken for his editing skill and his organizational abilities in getting the publication to press.

Myra Green and Richard McClintock jumped in early in the process with their editing and grammatical skills. Hours were freely given and generously poured into each manuscript draft. Richard McClintock also contributed his graphic design skills in creating the book's cover.

Thank you to Susie Phillips and Greg Starbuck for giving wise counsel and able assistance.

To my amazing wife of thirty-three years, Karen, and our four wonderful children: Alec, Naomi, Faith, and Sharon, I am exceedingly grateful for your presence in my life. I thank Karen especially for surrounding me with unconditional love, thereby enabling me to fully trust in the healing power of genuine love.

And to God, my Father, for placing in my path those that would not let me fail: Mom and Dad Ball, Aunt Moe, Aunt Sweetheart and Grandma Brown, Darrell and Darlene Shirley, Mama Joyce and Daymond Helton, Vic Edwards, and so many others.

The Social Problem River

I WANT YOU TO IMAGINE you are a lifeguard. But I want you to imagine much more than that.

Imagine you have always dreamed of being a lifeguard. For as long as you can remember, that's all you ever wanted to be. Now your dream has come true. You are a trained, credentialed, and gainfully employed lifeguard.

Now pretend that this particular day happens to be your first holiday from work. Since you love the water so much, you decide to have a picnic down by a river that runs through your community. All is pleasant and well…until you hear the muffled, choking scream of a drowning child.

What are you going to do?

You haven't finished your lunch. It's your day off. The river is not your responsibility. Of course, none of that matters to you. You are a lifeguard—a lifeguard by training—a lifeguard by calling. Instinct and heart kick in and, like all first-responders, you naturally run towards the danger when others run away.

You dive in and swim out. You pull the helpless drowning child to the bank where you immediately perform CPR. She revives. You receive immediate and deeply satisfying affirmation of your choice of professions. What you dreamed of for so long has paid rich dividends for both you and the child you saved. It doesn't get any sweeter than that moment.

However, before you have much time to bask in the glory of it all, you hear the sounds of two children struggling to stay afloat near the same spot.

What are you going to do?

It's still your day off. You haven't fully regained your composure. It still isn't your responsibility. And now there are two.

You put on your best professional self and jump back in. You've been trained to rescue two at a time, and you're pleased to see you have remembered your training. After bringing both nearly dead children to shore, you do CPR on one, then the other. Checking periodically on the first victim, you keep this up until both new arrivals are breathing again on their own.

Exhausted, you aren't sure what you hear next. Maybe because you are so tired, the sounds you are hearing can't be real. But they are. You listen carefully. You make out the terrifying sounds of multiple victims. Once again instinct, and luckily a good dose of adrenaline, renews your strength. You quickly run to the water's edge. Assessing the situation, as you were taught to do before diving into the unknown, you count six little heads bobbing up and down in the swift current.

What are you going to do?

The circumstances haven't changed. It's still your day off. The river is not your responsibility. Besides three water-logged babes clinging desperately to your side, you are all alone. And now, the fact that you didn't finish your lunch is taking its toll.

What are you going to do?

You've not been trained to rescue so many by yourself; and there are no resources anywhere in sight to aid you in the daunting task now before you. But even if there were, it wouldn't matter much now. Because while you are standing there trying to decide on a plan, you see even more. Like a serial killer who takes sick pleasure in showing people the extent of his crimes, the river reveals to you even more of its casualties. In fact, it finally dawns on you that they must have been there all along, even as you leisurely enjoyed your day away. The roar that you thought was the sound of the river rushing by was the cries of countless children going down to an unthinkable fate. Guilt overwhelms you. But you have no time for that useless emotion.

For the first time today, you look upstream and to your horror all you can see are drowning and drowned children. Thousands, maybe even hundreds of thousands, of flailing children and lifeless bodies are rapidly passing downstream.

What are you going to do?

Obviously you need help, lots of help. You also need lots of resources and a game plan, a good strategy. You must find a way to do the most good for the most kids in the most efficient way possible. But you can't even grasp the extent of the problem! From your vantage point on the river's edge, you cannot tell how far this awful, ugly river runs in both directions. It may be so full of hopeless children that you could spend your entire lifetime camped out next to it and barely touch the problem.

What are you going to do?

The real question is—what are *we* going to do?

This river of social problems runs both deep and fast with multiple channels. New tributaries are constantly being added. Poverty, broken families, teen pregnancy, substance abuse, poor education, child abuse, neglect, and delinquency are just some of the currents flowing into this river. The tragic state of the modern child welfare system, once designed and built to save these children, is now a major contributor to the problem. Millions of vulnerable children are losing their struggle to keep their heads above water. A fallen and toxic culture is depriving them of a full and prosperous future, and in many cases, even of life itself. It's going to take a well-conceived and dedicated effort on the part of many people to empty this murderous river of its young victims.

What are we going to do?

There are many things we can do, more than we are currently doing. If we're going to make any real and lasting difference, we need the helping hands of trained professionals and volunteers, of experts and of regular citizens. With so much at stake we dare not limit the pool of possible helpers.

We need folks specially trained in all kinds of areas—from healthcare to fundraising, from social work to social media. We need lots of folks who are willing and able to pitch in wherever they can. We need people and we need resources. We need safety nets, flotation devices, boats, warning signs, even fences, because we need to do prevention as well as treatment if we are to solve the problem.

We need to know much more than we already know about how these kids got in the river. We need to go upstream and investigate the situation. We also need to be confident that we know enough to get started. And we must hurry! This is a Code Blue emergency. It requires focus, collaboration, teamwork, and urgency. Impatience in the service of vulnerable children is not a vice; it is a virtue. These precious little ones can't afford to wait for us adults to figure it all out before we act. They need help now!

There needs to be a great deal of hard work, for sure. Although it isn't really that difficult. Rescuing children and restoring the broken families and communities that discarded them into this dangerous river isn't all that complex or complicated. Common sense can go a long way on this particular waterway. Unfortunately, however, common sense is a rare commodity these days, and that is largely the issue.

This book is the account of my own unique, yet common, experience in that deadly river, both as a victim and as a rescuer. Some of its nasty water still remains in my lungs, affecting the way I think and live today. My time in and out of that river has undoubtedly biased my perspective. I believe, however, that my viewpoint may prove valuable.

Through this book I want to offer hope as well as solutions to this national nightmare. It's not meant to be a memoir of my entire life. Neither is it an academic treatise on all the social ills that negatively affect today's children. It is, however, a short telling of my own traumatic childhood and how I was rescued and healed. It is also an outline of a simple, common-sense strategy for how we can all work together to effectively save more children in distress, and maybe even stop that cursed river from flowing.

What are we going to do?

1

Rejected

One more time, and for the very last time,
my mother rejected me.

"Is Cora Wendel your mother?"

Instantly, I was engulfed by a familiar melancholy. My spirit became heavy. My stomach churned. I thought seriously about not replying. Big sigh....

"Yes. Why do you ask?"

The person on the other end of the Facebook Message identified herself and explained that she was a home healthcare nurse providing hospice services to my mother.

"Your mom is dying."

Crap! I knew I shouldn't have responded. Now it was too late.

It was May 2010, just a few weeks before I would become Executive Director of Patrick Henry Family Services, a ministry providing critical services to vulnerable children and distressed families. I was living in Goshen, Indiana, the heart of Amish country, with my wife and two of our four children who were still living at home. I had neither seen nor heard from my mother in nearly a decade. That had been perfectly fine with me. I was finally in a place in my life where I felt healed from my chaotic and abusive past. It had taken years and lots of inner turmoil to get there. That unexpected message revealed that I wasn't healed, at least not fully. There was one more thing I needed to do. I needed to write this book.

In her lifetime my mother carried the legal names of Cora Wood (her maiden name), Cora Brown, Cora Bray, Cora Day, and for the last twelve years or so, Cora Wendel. She had that one the longest, but I barely knew her by that name.

She was homeless, living in her car that no longer started, when she met Richard Wendel. He was chronically ill. They took care of each other. It was a relationship of mutual utility. I suppose that, in a sad kind of way, she was happiest during those last years. She was finally with a man who stayed (that is, until he died) and didn't abuse, cheat, or take advantage of her. I guess that's all she ever wanted. That's not asking for much. Yet for some reason it eluded my mother most of her life.

#332. A SACRED PRIVILEGE

Other than deciding to make a spiritual conversion and follow Christ with all our heart, soul, mind and strength, the single most important decision any human being can make is whom to marry.

Think about it. Choosing the wrong spouse can have all kinds of long-term negative consequences. It can lead to an onslaught of pain and loss, including, but not limited to, harm to children, financial bankruptcy, emotional and physical trauma, spiritual deformity, broken relationships, misguided careers, lost passions, and even stolen identities — a stolen identity of who you were intended to be in Christ.

Unfortunately our society has become far too careless about this decision. Without a devout commitment to seeking the kind of love God created us for, we run the risk of settling for a cheap counterfeit, never experiencing the fullness of love. We must get back to the place where we treat matrimony as the most sacred privilege on this side of heaven.

StraightTalkwithRobertDay.org

There were a lot more names during her sixty-five years. A woman with little education, few skills, and a big gaping hole in her heart will have many paramours, just in order to survive physically and emotionally. My mother had more in her life than I can remember or count. As you can probably imagine, they weren't the best of men, although they included a prominent business leader, a state senator, and a few other "good catches." But those relationships had pretty short expiration dates. Their wives made sure of it.

As an adult, I have had the occasion of meeting some of these men while doing business or at a community function. None of them remember me, or at least suggest in any way that they do. I don't bring it up, but I remember them. I especially recall the promises some of them made to me as a child, promises they never kept nor probably ever had any intentions of keeping. They were the sort of pledges men on the hunt make to the children of women they're after, empty words designed to make everyone feel wanted. They are the worst kind of lies men use to manipulate single mothers.

There were times when we were out of food, or the rent was past due, that my mother would give me a dime and a telephone number. I would find a public payphone and call the number, which she had usually written on my hand or forearm. When the person answered I simply said, "Cora needs money." A man would eventually show up and spend the night. Crisis averted.

If my mother was with a guy for any stretch of time, she would unofficially take on his last name. She made sure I did as well. That is, if I was part of the picture. Most of the time I wasn't. I can remember getting into an argument once with a teacher who told me that the name I was signing on my papers was not my legal name. He insisted that I stop. I insisted otherwise. He lost. You see, I had to choose whether to do as he said or do what my mother wanted. I knew that I wasn't likely to be in that school for long, and the man with the different last name wasn't likely to be around much longer.

So it really didn't matter. I continued to sign my name Bobby Hill until circumstances changed.

If you added up all the time I lived with my mother, just the two of us, without the presence of some unrelated man, it would probably be less than six months total. That was good though. Because those few times were the worst. During those periods I was basically on my own and fending for myself.

When my mother was married or living with someone, I was not normally around. With the exception of my adoptive father, I usually lived somewhere else — sometimes close by, sometimes not; sometimes with relatives, sometimes not; sometimes in good situations, sometimes not. Actually, a lot of times not.

That was the way she liked it, though. I was usually close enough that if she wanted or needed me, she could get her hands on me (usually to show the caseworker I existed) but far enough away not to get in the way of her love life. She told me more than once, in no uncertain terms, that she would pick her new husband or boyfriend over me if it came to that. I knew, by experience, she was serious.

As a result of my mother's wandering ways and unstable relationships, I lived in over thirty different places before I graduated from high school. Very few I would call home. None would be any longer than two years.

"Next time my mother is conscious, ask her if her firstborn can come see her."

After I was born, my mother had four other sons from her first marriage. They had not been a part of her life since they were very young. I asked if her firstborn could visit as a gentle reminder to her that she had other children, and they might want to know she was dying. I had been conditioned as a child to avoid saying to my mother what I really meant. When I did there was usually hell to pay. Forty-nine years old, married and with kids of my own, I couldn't believe I so easily reverted back to "gentle" reminders. Part of it was due to the passive-aggressive nature of my Appalachian culture. Part of it was due to my conflict-avoidant type of personality. Mostly, though, I was couching the question in such a way as to soften the blow of what I was pretty certain would be her answer.

"Your mother was conscious today. We had a good talk. I told her that I have been in contact with you. I asked if you could visit her. She said no. Fred [not his real name] said he would kill you if you showed up down here."

After Richard Wendel passed away, my mother shacked up one last time with an old mountain man I didn't know. I wasn't surprised though. She couldn't be without a man for very long... except me.

It wasn't his threat that bothered me. I couldn't have cared less about him or the stuff he thought I would want to take after her death. I was certain she had nothing I desired except maybe a handful of tattered photos she kept scattered in a shoebox, and those weren't worth the drama. It was my mother's answer that stung. It was why I didn't want to reply to the initial message. One more time, and for the very last time, my mother rejected me. It hurt...again.

Because unconditional acceptance and affirmation are so vital to the emotional health of a child, I am convinced that rejection from a parent is probably the deepest and longest lasting emotional wound a child can ever suffer. Dr. Frank Lake, one of the pioneers of pastoral counseling, said, "children descend into hell when love is squeezed out of them by parental neglect."

Those who have been abandoned or rejected, by their mother in particular, feel the added heartache of being robbed of something innately sacrosanct. It is a silent, simmering kind of pain that leaves the person in an altered state. If not dealt with properly, it can be destructive to the one rejected and even to those they try to love.

Without some professional help and divine healing, a person will likely spend his or her entire life trying to overcome that hurt. I sought both, and in time received relief from the ache and achieved some sense of normalcy. The second part of my life story recounts my rocky journey towards healing and explains the process needed to be whole.

I can honestly say today that I hold no ill will in my heart against my mother. There's no more hidden anger or deep-rooted bitterness. My inner child is fine. On the other hand, there isn't any great love either. On the matter of my mother, I feel neutral. Trust me — it's perfectly okay and even healthy to feel neutral in such cases. Don't let anyone, especially yourself, put you on a guilt trip for not feeling more.

As a grown adult with children of my own, and working in a helping profession, I have come to understand that my mother's many deficits were imparted to her by her severely dysfunctional family and by living in a culture of deep and pervasive poverty. As I reflect on the many bad choices she made during her life, I try to keep that in perspective. It helps to remember that she also grew up without a father and with a mother who was similarly unattached. That does not absolve her of her sinful choices or of the pain she caused. It does, however, put her deeds in a context of the trauma and pain she experienced herself. In other words, she was a victim as much as a villain. Perhaps if she had received help, things would have been markedly different for both of us.

Another message came about a week later.

"Your mother passed away today. I'll let you know about the arrangements."

I thanked her for letting me know and said I had no interest in attending the funeral. I did not shed a single tear that day or any day since. That's not to say I didn't mourn, though. I did and I still do. I persistently despair the loss of never really having a mother.

Some of you can relate. The sadness of never having been truly loved by a parent bestows a tenacious sense of loneliness. Even in a crowd of people I know, and dear friends and family I cherish, a shadow of insecurity sometimes lingers just beneath the surface as if taunting me: "You have nothing to be happy about. No one loves you; they're all going to leave you."

Maybe you think I'm callous. The hospice nurse certainly did. She couldn't believe that I didn't drop everything and rush to Tennessee to be by my mother's side. But I know that some of you reading this will understand. For folks like us, Mother's Day is the toughest holiday of the year. We can honor motherhood as a beautiful concept and highest ideal, but we cannot sincerely celebrate our own mothers.

A mother's love is considered a universal constant. It is settled science, so to speak. Sure, it's accepted that a father may be absent or present and cold. Friends aren't always reliable, even the best of friends. And love between a husband and wife might fade with time or circumstances. But a mother's love is thought to be unconditional and without end. That idea is simply unquestioned by the majority of the population. A mother's love is lifted up as the highest of earthly virtues. But it isn't reality for millions of people. We would rather trade every holiday on the calendar for the chance to have a mother we can honor and celebrate.

In the end, I did go to the funeral. I learned that Joe, the oldest of my four younger brothers, was going, and I wanted desperately to see him. He needed closure and I guess I did too. We met each other in Tennessee. He came from Iowa, I from Indiana. We hugged and sat together in silence and observed the lifeless body of the one who gave birth to us.

My mother had always been an attractive woman. In her younger days she had been given the nickname Sam. It was short for Samantha, the main character on the television show *Bewitched*, whom many swore she resembled. Getting the attention of suitors was not a problem for my mother. But the woman lying in eternal rest didn't look anything at all like her. She had always lived hard. But her last years had obviously been very difficult. I looked closely for something that assured me this was indeed my mother.

I couldn't find it. The lady in the casket was a stranger to me, in more ways than one.

It was the most pitiful funeral I've ever attended, and as a pastor I have been to a good number of them. It's true what they say, that you can tell a lot about a person's life by how she is buried. The place was nearly empty. No one rose to give a testimony about her life. None of her eight remaining siblings were present. The pallbearers were hired. I was pleased to see my adoptive father (her third husband) there, but the only one who seemed to be truly grieving her passing was the old mountain man. Unshaven, dressed in well-worn bib overalls and wrinkled white shirt, he sobbed throughout the service and never left her side. When the service was over I embraced the man who had earlier threatened to kill me and told him I was sorry for his loss.

After the service Joe and I (along with my dear cousin, Will Jones, and my son, Alec, who had both come to provide support) went to the place where my brother and I lived together briefly with our three other siblings before we were permanently separated. I was nine at the time. He was only seven. Although the structure no longer stood, he recognized the spot instantly. It had been nearly forty years since we lived at that address, but the memories were palpable for both of us. Neither of us had gotten emotional at the funeral, but there, at this nondescript spot on the side of the road, standing together on an empty concrete pad, the tears flowed freely.

My brother and I shared a strange bond. It was the sort of connection that people who suffer together or experience the same tragedy have with one another. Even though we hadn't seen each other in years, on that day and in that empty space, we were chained together to the same foul memories. It felt like we were children again, but not in a good way. We felt exposed and vulnerable just as we did four decades earlier.

It was the fall of 1971 when Everett Brown, my mother's first husband, unexpectedly showed up and abducted his four boys but left me standing on the side of the road.

A couple of months before, my twenty-six-year-old mother had filed for divorce, packed up all five of her children (including me living somewhere else), and moved back to Jellico, her ancestral home, a small coal town on the border of Tennessee and Kentucky. As many times as we moved, we always bounced back to Jellico. I would eventually graduate from there, and despite living in so many different places, consider it my first hometown.

The town's unofficial motto — "No matter where you go, you'll meet someone from Jellico" — says everything you need to know about it. In its heyday, though, when coal was king, it was a thriving community with an opera house that produced singer Grace Moore. At one time it had a larger population than Knoxville. Johnny Cash even mentions it in his song "I've Been Everywhere Man." By the 1970s it was struggling, and has ever since the government built more public housing than the small community could sustain. The uncanny ability of distant, centralized planners to ruin the lives of individuals, families, and even entire communities never ceases to amaze me.

The father of my four brothers (Joe, David, Randy, Leslie) found the little two-bedroom apartment over an auto repair shop on the main road where we had been living all summer. School had recently started when he arrived. He and his brother had staked out the place the day before and slept in his car nearby.

That unhappy abode was provided to us courtesy of the greasy shop owner whom we would often see in the afternoons. We knew the routine. He would walk in without knocking. We would go to our bedroom and remain there for hours, sometimes until the next day or even the day after that. We were always given clear instructions not to make any noise.

There was no air conditioning and we would burn up during the day from the heat in that locked room. With no toys and nothing to do but wait, we fought like wild dogs. Joe and I would sometimes go at each other with every intent to do great bodily harm. We punched, scratched, kicked, gouged, and bit the hours and days away. My mother would come in screaming and whip all of us with a switch or a belt. It didn't matter if you were guilty of the crime of making noise or not. Everyone got a few lashes on the bare legs and back for good measure.

If she was in an especially cruel mood she would have us pick out our own instrument of abuse. She liked thin green branches with a lot of bend to them and would get more upset if we didn't bring her a proper switch to use on us. We would start crying and pleading with her the moment she told us to "go cut me a good switch so I can whip your noisy ass." If we hesitated, we got slapped in the face until we started moving in the right direction.

I believe in corporal discipline (not punishment) and in a parent's right to practice it, but this was clearly child abuse. First of all, the punishment (not discipline) didn't fit the crime and was intended to induce fear as well as pain. Secondly, using an object to strike a child and leave injury is the very definition of abuse. In fact, if she did it to any other person, child or adult, she could have been prosecuted for Assault and Battery with an object. No parent has a right to abuse his or her children for any reason, and no child should have to endure such brutish treatment, even by a parent.

At night, though, we boys put our strife aside, and because the two single mattresses on the floor had no covering, and because we were usually dressed in only our underwear, we would huddle together to keep warm. All of us on one bed. Joe and I would sleep on the edges with our little brothers in the middle. I'll let you imagine what it smelled like in that tiny room.

When we weren't locked in our bedroom, we would play in the parking lot among the broken-down cars waiting to be fixed. I guess that is how we got the attention of Social Services. Someone must have reported the sights and sounds coming from that apartment and the five pitiful urchins who lived there. Social Services dutifully notified Everett Brown in Iowa that they were going to place us in foster care if things didn't get better quickly.

As a former Child Protective Services worker for the State of Alaska, I look back at that situation and wonder why it took so long. Some of the explanation may be found in the date. That happened just a few years before the Child Abuse Prevention and Treatment Act (CAPTA) was passed in 1974, providing clear definitions of abuse and neglect, naming mandated reporters, and setting strict time frames for investigating reports of harm to children.

Everett Brown and his brother made their daring move in the early morning while my brother Joe and I were waiting for the school bus in front of Ray Maiden's old store. We were about a hundred yards up the street from where we shared our prison cell. Just days before, my clever brother had learned how to get his arm through the distribution end of a Coke machine and grab a can of pop. Since none of the rest of us could do it, he happily dispensed free sodas to anyone who asked, which, of course, was everyone. That freebie, though, would end that day.

To our great surprise and joy, Everett Brown pulled up next to us and told Joe to hurry up and get in the car. He happily obeyed. I started to get in, too, but the man who I thought at the time was my father told me he couldn't take me. Years later he told me that leaving me there on the side of the road was the hardest thing he had ever done. He explained that taking me would have been considered kidnapping, and he couldn't risk losing the other boys.

I thought at the time that he meant there was no room in the car, so I started walking back to the apartment so excited to see him again. I thought it was going to be a special day. Before I could get there, however, I saw my barely-clothed mother shouting and swearing and chasing after Everett Brown, who had the other three boys, the youngest just an infant in his arms. Once back home in Iowa it was discovered that my youngest brother Leslie was gravely ill and could have perished if he had remained in that apartment for much longer.

Everett Brown put all his boys in the car and sped off as fast as he could. My mother went chasing down the road after them like a crazy woman. When she saw it was futile, she stopped yelling but kept running until she got to her mother's house about a half mile down the state highway. Puzzled by what had just occurred and not sure what I was supposed to do, I followed after her as quickly as my nine-year-old legs could run. Embarrassed by the spectacle, I slowed down to a walk as my school bus passed with the faces of my peers pressed hard against the windows of the bus, curious to know what happened.

I would not see my four brothers again until 1998, twenty-seven years later. Despite the intentions of Child Protective Services, matters went from bad to worse for me.

Even though it was painful and a bit awkward, I'm so glad I joined my long-lost brother at our mother's funeral. Weary of life's struggles and hardships, he committed suicide about a year later. That awful river claimed another victim. It has the power to do that, even when they are no longer children.

The other brothers gave me the unpleasant honor of officiating at his funeral in Iowa. The life of this former Marine and ex-felon with a big heart was celebrated by a packed house of friends and family members. It was the rowdiest funeral I've ever witnessed.

Even though I barely knew him as an adult, I had no trouble crying that day for the little boy I remembered. Not so much because he was dead, but because he died never having known that which I believe he longed for so desperately—the unconditional love and unquestionable acceptance of his own mother. I can't think of anything more unnaturally tragic. Can you?

What are we going to do?

2
Taken

No! I love you even more than that!

THERE WERE TWO painful messages I heard throughout my childhood. Both still echo in my head from time to time. When they do, I take them captive and submit them to the light of the truth. Unfortunately, it took me a while to learn how to do that.

"You know, I put you up for adoption when you were born."

Hearing it once would be enough to plant the seed of doubt and shame in a young child. I heard it often enough to know what she was really saying to me. Let me tell you about the first time I was rejected by my mother, and the first woman to take her place and love me unconditionally as a mother should.

Early in 1961, my mother was sixteen years old and newly pregnant. According to what I have been able to piece together, including her own account, my mother was riding in the back seat of a car going down a narrow mountain road in Tennessee. Her mother and her mother's boyfriend were in the front seat. (The driver may have been my mother's father, but I don't know. My mother was always evasive about that). The pair were drinking moonshine and headed for trouble.

I know from experience that my maternal grandmother was a "mean drunk." She weighed about 300 pounds, so it took a lot of liquor (not as much moonshine, which she loved) for her to get "good-n-drunk." But when she did consume enough alcohol of any kind, she became belligerent and violent.

My Grandma Wood had a malicious reputation and few, including most men, would tangle with her. In fact, I would use that common bit of knowledge to my advantage when needed. As a boy I would throw her name about if I wanted someone to back off. I did that once with someone who was acting hostile and mouthing threats. His demeanor quickly changed as he told me that my grandmother nearly killed his cousin in a bar fight. My grandmother gave me "hollow cred" (like "street cred" but useful only in the mountains and hollows of Appalachia).

As the story goes, my grandmother and her mystery companion were traveling down the road with my pregnant adolescent mother in the backseat. They came upon another vehicle heading in the opposite direction. That is when something atrocious occurred.

Neither driver wanted to back up to the nearest wide spot to allow the other to pass. An argument broke out between the two drivers. The argument became a fight. The other driver's throat was slashed and his bloody body thrown over a cliff to his death. The only thing I know for certain after this point in the ghastly story is that my mother became a ward of the state and was placed in an unwed mothers' home in Nashville.

Pregnant teens weren't mainstreamed back then like they are today, and there certainly weren't television shows encouraging it in the name of "reality." The shame of it provided some negative social reinforcement that had some positive outcomes. We have lost that now.

It was while she was in that group home that I was born.

Eventually, she was placed in a foster home back in the eastern part of the state. For the first and only time in my mother's life, she had a stable and safe place to live. She was in a Christian home with a loving couple who took her as their own child and gave her opportunities she neither had before nor would ever have again. Regrettably, that wouldn't be enough for her.

Children who grow up in environments where chaos is the norm often don't know what to do when things are actually normal. Sometimes they subconsciously throw things off balance, create a little chaos or drama, in order to feel better. We see it all the time at Patrick Henry Boys and Girls Homes. Many of the children in our care will sabotage their own success, and they can be pretty creative about it.

There is a growing body of evidence that suggests childhood abandonment leads to self-sabotage in adulthood as well. Unhappily, I've seen it plenty of times in my own life and can give anecdotal confirmation of its reality.

Even as an adult, I lived out behaviors I learned from my dysfunctional mother. Just as things would settle into predictable routines, I would get an itch to change things or move. When you change addresses as often as I did, staying in one place for more than a couple of years feels unnatural. Just when I was reaching some level of success in a job, I would do something to ruin it. I would do it in a way that looked like it was something that happened to me, leaving me no choice but to move on. When you grow up constantly being victimized, it is very easy to play the role of the victim because it is a familiar, comfortable known quantity. It's like breathing. Most of the time you are not aware you are doing it.

It wasn't until I found a measure of healing that I recognized what I was doing to myself and to my poor wife and children. I had to get to an emotional state of being in which it was acceptable, even preferable, for me to allow good things to happen. I had to get to a point where it felt fine to stay in one place. I thank the Lord for my dear family who loved me through a few of these negative cycles before things got better. To learn more about that part of my story and how I found healing, read *Pealing Away the Past*.

My mother's foster parents, George and JoAnne Ball, were everything you would want in foster parents. They didn't have much in terms of material possessions, barely making a living on a patch of rocky farm land. But they were honest, hard-working people who loved the Lord, truly "salt of the earth" types. They provided all the essentials for a good life and were generous in their attention and affection.

They were older and unable to have children of their own. In time, they decided to be foster parents to fulfill their personal longing for children, and because they believed God called them to the important ministry of caring for orphans. My mother was their first placement. Because she broke their heart, she was their only foster child.

Mom Ball and Dad Ball, as my mother called them, requested that the State also place me with them, and about ten weeks later I arrived. When I started talking, the story goes, I called my mother "Sis" because that's how they addressed her. In their eyes we were both their children. It was their desire to adopt me; however, I have never learned why that didn't happen. It's reasonable to assume that my mother changed her mind for some reason and didn't want to relinquish her parental rights.

When my mother turned eighteen she made a fateful decision that I have regretted my entire life. Although she had a safe place with people who were committed to her for the long haul, she left their orderly home and dismissed the positive future they offered. It was her legal right as an adult; nonetheless it devastated the Balls. My mother added insult to injury when she also took me with her. I have often wondered what it would have been like to grow up in one home with a godly family who loved me without question. Sadly that was not my fate. Instead, I was raised by an emotionally damaged child.

I had the worst of mothers, but because I had the worst of mothers, I also had the best of moms.

We now know from years of research that the first three years of a child's life are critical to his development. I'm so thankful that Mom Ball gave me a healthy start. The nurture she provided might have been the single greatest difference in my life. Without it, there might have been damage I could never overcome. It is believed, and there is strong evidence to support it, that every dollar a state government spends on early childhood intervention, making sure infants and toddlers are safe, healthy, and nurtured, will save eight dollars later on remedial services that have fewer positive outcomes.

I am also cognizant that I may owe my health and success today to the State of Tennessee. The simple fact that my mother was in state care during most of her pregnancy probably saved me from irrevocable harm. I was protected in the womb from drugs and alcohol that my mother could have, and probably would have, used if she hadn't been taken into custody because of an event that involved heavy drinking.

When my mother became an adult, she moved a thousand miles away to Sioux City, Iowa, to live with her older brother in an efficiency apartment above a gas station where he worked. He had moved there to get away from the craziness of the Wood family and the poverty of the mountains. He was part of the great migration from Appalachia to the northern states that Michael Harrington, in his book *The Other America*, referred to as the "great brain drain."

It was that book, more than any other, that made the poor of Appalachia visible to the rest of the nation. It gave inspiration to President Kennedy's concept of a Great Society and later President Johnson's War on Poverty. The "great brain drain" referred to the mass exodus from Appalachia after World War II in response to mass layoffs in the coal industry. Those with any skills, talent, or initiative went north on the "hillbilly highway" to look for a better life. Many northern cities still have sections predominately made up of Appalachia people. The migration stopped abruptly in 1965 with the implementation of anti-poverty programs.

Like many others who fled the mountains in those days, my mother's brother wanted to make a good life for himself. He offered to help my mother do the same. It was while we were in Sioux City living with my Uncle Jay (from whom I got my middle name) that she met and married Everett Brown.

I will never really understand why she deserted what she knew for something she didn't. I will never fully comprehend why she took me away from Mom and Dad Ball, who loved me and wanted me as their own. If she had ever been honest enough to admit it, she too would have said it was a mistake. She certainly showed it often enough by her actions. Many times I have pondered what life would have been like if I had been adopted by my foster parents.

But wishful thinking doesn't change anything. Time is a funny thing, isn't it? It only goes forward. Rather than worrying and fretting about what did or didn't happen in my past, I hold firm to the hope that is in me because of the future I have been given in Christ.

#25. Future Possibilities

I am going to let you in on a secret. What you think about your future is much more important to your success than what you think about your past. That is just the opposite of what most people have been led to believe. Psychologists like to focus on a person's past to explain behavior. Sociologists like to focus on a person's present environment to explain behavior. But I am here to tell you that neither one is correct.

Take a troubled child with an abusive past, give that child hope that the future can be different, and that child will be successful. But if you take the same child and focus on his past, you will only create a victim whose future will be little more than a repeat of his miserable past.

Helping troubled kids see the possibilities of the future is a much better way of helping them than giving them a bunch of psychobabble about their past. Trust me, I know.

StraightTalkwithRobertDay.org

It is the general consensus that few adults can remember anything that happened to them prior to age three. But I have distinct memories of my time on the Balls' little farm. For a while in my childhood I was confused about the timeline and the people in those memories. Conversations over the years with the key figures helped me to understand that the earliest memories I have, hidden deep in the recesses of my mind and heart, took place within the loving confines of that home.

I can remember feeding the pigs with Mom Ball, probably because they frightened me. I can remember Dad Ball taking me to get my very first haircut. The adults in the barber shop teased me because I looked like a girl. I had long curly blond hair before the barber's scissors were let loose on my head. After that haircut, I had neither curls nor blond hair again. Mom Ball cried about that. My mother confirmed that story more than once.

There is an event pressed firmly in my memory. Mom Ball left me in a playpen in the yard. I watched intently as she walked away and then came back leading a calf by a rope. I also clearly recall another moment of being scared and crying at a barking dog at our screened door, and of Dad Ball lovingly taking me up into his arms where I felt safe.

Tears still stir in my eyes when I think of the sweetest of all the memories on the farm. My most precious memory is of Mom Ball holding me in her lap and playing that cute game that nurturing parents sometimes play with their children. Holding her thumb and pointer finger an inch apart she said, "Do I love you this much? No." Holding two hands a foot apart, "Do I love you this much? No." Holding her two hands as far apart as she could, she asked one more time, "Do I love you *this much?* NO! I LOVE YOU EVEN MORE THAN THAT!"

I can also remember the sad day I was taken from that farm.

There is something, though, that exists even deeper than memory. It's more akin to an intuition than a remembrance. If the mind can bury all recollection of traumatic abuse, can it not also store up feelings of love and security that the individual can draw upon during bad times? I think so. There were definite memories of a special place and of wonderful people who loved me, but it was the sweet emotions associated with them that lingered throughout my childhood. When I needed them most I withdrew them like money from a savings account. My Mom Ball made sure I had enough in that account that I would never run out.

The second persistent message I heard from my mother: "I swear you must have been switched at birth. You can't be mine."

I never felt a bond with my mother. I'm not sure why. Perhaps because she abandoned me at birth and we didn't have a physical connection at that critical opportune time. Perhaps because I had some kind of spiritual or emotional association with the Balls that made her jealous. Or perhaps I really was switched at birth. I do know this for sure, with only two exceptions—I never felt secure or at home during my entire childhood. This was especially true when I lived with her. I was a fish in a desert.

My mother and I had nothing in common. I didn't like any of the things she liked. I didn't really enjoy being with her. I always felt on guard around her. I never felt fully comfortable in her presence. I'm sure she sensed that uneasiness from me and it played a role in her many acts of rejection. But I also discerned the same uneasiness coming from her, which then caused me not to invest fully in the relationship.

Based on what we know today about bonding, I might have been diagnosed as having Reactive Attachment Disorder (RAD). However, I think that would be wrong, because I didn't have any problems attaching to many of my other substitute caregivers. In fact, my ability to get adults to like me is how I survived. I realize that it's much more complicated than I am making it out here. However, I fear that many children today are receiving treatment for RAD when it is their caregivers (birth, step, foster, or adoptive) who have the true bonding issue.

After getting into trouble with Social Services and losing four of her children to the legal custody of Everett Brown (and a failed relationship with my real father, which you'll read about in chapter four), my mother took me to stay with the foster parents who had prayed for me every day I was away from them. They asked the Lord for a chance to see me again and he answered their prayers. I was returned to Mom and Dad Ball. I was brought back to my first home.

My time there was truly special. I'm uncertain how long I was there the second time. Those early years of the 70s in the Cumberland Mountains of Tennessee and Kentucky were so chaotic that I can't get all the places and events in proper sequence. Yet I do know this—it wasn't nearly long enough.

Mom and Dad Ball were old enough to be my grandparents, but they did everything within their power and resources to be what I needed them to be. They made sure I was in church every time the doors were open. Mom Ball's brother was the pastor of the Baptist church we attended. I have many pleasant recollections of Sunday School, Vacation Bible School, and Sunday afternoons at Uncle Don's. The first movement of God in my heart was at that country church.

Like many other churches in those days, they showed a poorly produced Christian filmed titled *The Burning Hell*. It purportedly depicted the fate of those who did not receive Jesus as their savior. It scared me enough to walk forward during the invitation. Thankfully that wasn't the only thing that got my attention or moved me spiritually. The love and grace of the congregation grounded me in another, more positive, way.

They no longer lived on the farm. They had moved closer to town, near LaFollettee, Tennessee. Dad Ball was tall and lanky. He always sported a flat top and was part of that generation of men who liked wearing their pants above the belly button. He worked hard as a mechanic at a feed and grain warehouse. I loved going with him to the warehouse and playing among the giant stacks of feed bags and smelling the different grains. He made sure I learned how to mow the grass and take care of the yard. People think I'm a little OCD about cutting the grass, but it's because I do it "right," the way Dad Ball taught me.

While Dad Ball was trying to teach me to be responsible, Mom Ball spoiled me. Unlike Dad Ball, she was short and a little chubby. She liked wearing her hair up in a bun. That required a weekly appointment at the hairdresser's. Her horn-rimmed glasses could not take away from her beautiful smile. When I was in her care I ate pretty much what I wanted, as much as I wanted, when I wanted. Once I ate an entire loaf of bread and a jar of peanut butter for an after-school snack. She didn't try to stop me. I left my toys all over the house but my clothes always had to be folded and put away. As long as my toys weren't in the way of her watching *The Waltons* and *The Lawrence Welk Show*, it was okay with her.

Don't get me wrong. There was plenty of discipline as well. They didn't put up with any hint of disrespect, laziness, or talking during worship service. They also held to an old family lore that children should wear their winter coats until the trees on top of the mountains are in full bloom. Not only did this make me unnecessarily hot on a lot of spring days, but I also looked pretty foolish going to school on warm, sunny days in my winter coat.

I can remember many evenings after supper, the two of them trying their best to help me with my homework. It was the first and only time in my education that any of my caregivers did that. I regret that I gave them such fits, thus sabotaging my own success.

They ushered me through my first case of puppy love. They were patient and gave age-appropriate advice. In contrast, the first time I told my mother about a girl I liked, she asked if I had protection. I told her I had a pocket knife if I needed it. She laughed and handed me a condom.

Before my first crush on a girl, Dad Ball had tried to explain to me about the birds and bees. He told me that boys who like girls were heterosexuals and that boys who like other boys were homo-sexuals. I had just turned eleven. Since I didn't like girls at the time I thought that meant I was a homosexual. I went to school the next day and proclaimed to all my friends that I was a homosexual. They thought it would be cool to have a homosexual club that didn't allow girls. They made me president. It was my first practice in leadership. When I returned home from school and proudly told Dad Ball what had happened, he just smiled and told me to come see him when I started liking girls.

Later, I think I was fourteen, my mother accused me of being gay because I hadn't had sex yet, as she had at the same age. She also went on to claim that it would be proof enough I wasn't hers. I sometimes wondered if it would be better if I were gay—that way there would at least be some reason that I could connect to her serial rejection of me.

At night, the Balls would tuck me into bed with a little poem I'm sure you have heard before: "Night, night, sleep tight, don't let the bedbugs bite." They would take turns praying with me. Both would kiss me goodnight. Regrettably, this happy, idyllic situation was destined to be short-lived.

Though they hoped I might stay, they feared their time with me would be short, so they poured everything into me they could, from good food to Bible verses. They knew I would need it. My mother would come by occasionally, joining us for church or din-ner. I'm confident they were fervently praying for her to get her life on the right track.

At some point my mother found a job and a place to live, cer-tainly with the help and encouragement of the Balls, and took me with her. In one of the few photos I have of them, they visited us at the trailer park. I don't look well or happy. I wasn't. Things had deteriorated rapidly, as my mother was returning to her old ways.

Eventually she must have had a huge disagreement with them and kept them away. Over the years I would see them from time to time and sometimes talk by phone, but I was aware things would never be the same. Maybe they were trying to protect themselves from being hurt so much again. I don't know. There is no doubt in my mind, however, that they kept the promise they made to me on the day I was taken from them the second time: "We will continue to pray for you every day."

I was in college when Dad Ball died. I was driving by then and went to support Mom Ball. She held on tight to me throughout the service. She insisted I give him a kiss goodnight. I had no compulsion to but did because it meant so much to her. She loved us both deeply. It was a horribly hard day.

I was still in college when Mom Ball passed away. Both died from the same preventable cause—cigarettes. It was their only obvious weakness. I made some excuse that I couldn't attend her funeral, but to be truthful, I didn't have the inner strength to go. I regret very much that I didn't. I know she forgives me.

The landlord eventually kicked us out of the trailer where my mother had tried to make a fresh start. From there we moved into the basement of the tavern in Caryville, Tennessee, where my mother served drinks and undoubtedly met more losers.

It was an open, unfinished cinderblock basement. Most of the space was used to store old furniture, beer signs, and extra cases of beer. There were two cots in one corner with a black and white TV sitting on a folding chair. With bunny ears we could pick up two stations from Knoxville. Both were pretty fuzzy. Our clothes were in boxes under the beds. We used the public bathrooms upstairs in the bar. I could hear the jukebox playing late into the night and the many varied sounds of people drinking too much. I ate a lot of pizza, pickled bologna, and pork rinds, and drank a lot of Dr. Pepper for dinner and breakfast. Fortunately I had lunch at my new school.

Sometime in the middle of the night my mother would come to bed. She would sleep most of the next day, usually getting up about the time I got off the school bus. On the weekends, I played in the

parking lot when I got bored of bouncing a rubber ball off the basement walls. Sometimes I would just sit on the hillside overlooking
Interstate 75 and watch the traffic, wondering about the lives of the
people in the cars. I would soon turn twelve.

I can remember one day after school, lying on my cot watching
the television, when a woman I didn't know came walking down
the stairs. I sat up. She came over and began asking me a lot of
questions. I answered them honestly. I didn't know not to. After
making several notes on a notepad, she asked where my belongings
were and I pointed to the box under my bed. She grabbed my stuff
and asked me to follow her. We went upstairs and walked through
the sparsely crowded beer joint and out the front door.

I saw my mother in a corner at one of the tables surrounded by
some folks who all seemed to be conspiring together about something. I kept looking over at her waiting to catch her eye, but she
never looked my way. The woman, I assume a social worker, told me
that my mother knew where I was going and that everything was
going to be all right. She put me in the backseat of her car and drove
me over Jellico Mountain to the one place I dreaded most—the
squalid residence of my Grandmother Wood, my mother's hateful
mother. In rather short order, I went from the joys of heaven to the
deepest despairs of hell, with a brief stop in purgatory.

I learned early on that life's not always fair, or just, or good,
or kind, and there's little I can do about it. Later in life I learned
that while life may not be any of those things, I can be. It's a lesson I have no doubt George and JoAnne Ball tried to instill in me
through their life, love, and prayers for me. I think they would be
pleased at the outcome of their efforts.

What are we going to do?

3
Abused

A compliant child in a vulnerable situation
is an easy target for abuse and exploitation.

M Y MOTHER WAS THE SECOND oldest of eleven children (thirteen if you count two stillbirths) who grew up in abject poverty. By that I mean the third-world kind of hardship that was so
common in the mountains and hollows of Appalachia, America's
white ghetto, in those days prior to the War on Poverty. Imagine
all the worst stereotypes of uneducated, violence-prone, incestuous
hillbillies living in their own filth and depravity, and you pretty
much have the repugnant portrait of my mother's background. No,
I'm not exaggerating. To better understand the depth and scope of
the poverty and immorality, read Harry Caudill's *Night Comes to
the Cumberland: A Biography of a Depressed Area*. It was published
two years after I was born.

"As hopelessness deepened, general morality was undermined.
The sexual mores of the mountaineer were never strict. While the
highlanders were never 'Tobacco Roaders' by any stretch of the
imagination, they have, on the other hand, never been Victorians.
They have taken a practical attitude toward sex and quite unasham-
edly behave as nature guides them. The illegitimate child—the
mountaineer's term is 'base born'—was never viewed with the
disdain accorded such unfortunates in other societies. The bastards
were altogether too numerous for such treatment to be practical....

Illegitimates made up a sizable percentage of the population and, though the circumstances of their birth sometimes called for off-color jokes, they were not seriously rejected or scorned.

"This tolerant attitude toward the facts of life brought an amazing reaction when the public assistance program began to dispense hard cash for the support of illegitimate children. Before the advent of Welfare, the 'wronged' mother had been compelled to swear out a bastardly warrant charging the man with paternity of her child and requesting the court to require him to pay her a monthly sum for the child's support. Now, to draw welfare for the child, the woman had to report that the identity of the father was unknown or that she no longer knew his whereabouts. In the deepening destitution of the coal counties, astonishing numbers of women resorted to illicit associations, illegitimate children and the certainty of welfare checks in preference to the uncertainty of the holy but penniless state of matrimony" (p. 285-286).

I know nothing of my maternal grandfather, or what his family or upbringing was like. I do know that my maternal grandmother grew up in the worst squalor and decay imaginable. Poverty was their lifeblood; ignorance was the air they breathed. On more than one occasion, I heard people refer to them as nasty "white trash."

One time I had the misfortune of staying with my great-grandmother for three days. Words cannot express the absolute spiritual darkness of that horrible place. I am not identifying my great-grandmother's family name of origin on purpose. What I describe here, or in other parts of the book, is not representative of all people in Appalachia. While harsh poverty is still prevalent in many parts, the region is populated by good, respectable people, many of whom helped me.

My great-grandmother's small, immensely filthy cabin consisted of three rooms and a covered front porch that was grossly uneven. The largest room was separated by sheets or blankets that served as dividers to make smaller areas where various people (family and strangers) slept. One naked light bulb hung by a cord in the center of the room. It provided more shadow than illumination. It wasn't difficult, though, to see, hear, or smell what took place on the other side of those cloth partitions. I saw enough during that stay to confirm what I had suspected on the other occasions I had visited there with my Grandma Wood. Incest and sexual abuse were the natural order of things.

The smallest room was absent of any furniture. The only light came from a small broken window. There was a hole in the partially rotted floor near the center of the room. The room served as the bathroom if going outside was too much trouble. Not everyone hit the hole, and sometimes the corners of the room served as urinals if the hole was otherwise occupied. The smell was unbearable, especially on a hot summer day.

An adolescent relative who lived there had recently given birth to her first child. (I've always suspected that the father of the child was her father.) One day everyone was visiting in the third room that served as a kind of kitchen when someone asked the whereabouts of the baby. Nobody seemed to know. Finally the new mother got up from where she had been sitting and I said, "There's the baby." The young mother had been sitting on the child for probably a good twenty minutes. The baby was sleeping in a box filled with used clothes. Some weeks later, that helpless infant "mysteriously" died.

My Iowa family (with Everett Brown) was poor, too, but in a different way. I have always made a distinction in my mind between being poor and living in poverty. To me it's not so much a matter of degree or an issue of cause but rather a condition of the spirit. Poverty is a state of mind. It's a spiritual condition more than it is a financial statement.

Poverty has its own culture, with an idiosyncratic language, a maimed psychology, and a crippling perspective of the world that are alien to the middle class minions running the antipoverty initiatives. They believe fixing the problem only requires money—lots of money. Nothing could be further from the truth. Compassion without expectation is enablement, and that breeds dependency. The foundation of any healthy relationship is reciprocity. Without it, there's no dignity, and dysfunction will fill the character vacuum it leaves behind.

Everett Brown's family was working-class poor. Alcoholism made them poorer than necessary. All the males were addicted. The females were not, and like so many women in that difficult situation, the burden of family responsibilities fell doubly on them. Yet that generation of Browns managed, despite much hardship and suffering from that awful disease, to generally remain an intact and loving family.

The Wood family, on the other hand, was poverty-stricken. Generations of vice and lechery had shattered that family into many unmendable pieces. They were more a loose collection of broken individuals, each one fighting for themselves, than they were a family unit.

The truth is, I didn't realize at the time that the Browns were as poor as they were.

After my mother married Everett Brown, we eventually moved to Kansas City, Missouri, where he had found work at a meatpacking plant. I have always loved pork chops. People think I'm nuts when I go to a nice steakhouse and order pork chops. We apparently ate a great deal of fresh meat he brought home from the plant, and pork chops were a staple.

For a long time I falsely believed he was employed at the place where coins are made (Federal Mint), because I once asked him what he did while he was gone all day and he said he made money. I actually thought he was the man on the dime. A young Everett Brown looked a lot like a young Franklin Roosevelt.

My mother had three more children in fairly quick succession while in Missouri. Then there were four boys to manage (another would come later back in Iowa). But apparently we weren't doing so well. My mother was not properly taking care of us, and my step-father asked his sister Doris, whose nickname to this day is Moe, to move in and help. Aunt Moe was younger than my mother, only a teenager at the time. She dropped out of school and became our full-time caregiver. Decades later, to her credit, after she raised her own two boys, she earned a GED. Aunt Moe didn't just take care of us. She loved us. If the ability to love and nurture children is a talent, then my Aunt Moe is an All-Star. As bad as my childhood was, it could have been substantially worse were it not for the good people God sent to fill in the gaps. Aunt Moe was one of those people.

The clearest memory of my time in Missouri took place on April 9, 1968 (although I wouldn't know the date or the significance of my experience until much later). Kansas City was one of thirty-seven cities in the United States that rioted after the assassination of Martin Luther King Jr. Unlike the other cities that rioted on April 4, Kansas City erupted on April 9, the day of his funeral. Five people were killed, at least twenty were hospitalized with serious injuries, and over one hundred were arrested.

I can vividly recall watching Aunt Moe from the window of our second floor apartment. She crossed the street to use a payphone. She was attempting to call her family to let them know we were all right. I remember seeing soldiers pull up next to the phone booth and put her in their jeep and drive away. I also distinctly remember my eyes burning so badly that I started crying. So did my brothers. I remember Everett Brown putting us all in the shower together fully clothed and turning on the water to wash the teargas from our faces. It was pretty frightening. We did not understand what was happening to us at the time. Aunt Moe returned that evening as we were going to bed. She had been removed from the street as a safety precaution and was released when the riots ended.

Some time after that event, we packed up and moved back to Sioux City, home of Palmer Candy and their famous cherry Bing, which I hoard any chance I get. My mother, Everett Brown, and my brothers moved into a house together. Aunt Moe and I moved into the four-room shack belonging to Grandma and Grandpa Brown on Athone Avenue, along with their youngest son and daughter, whom I called Aunt Sweetheart. Six people were jammed into an eight-hundred-square-foot house. It was there that the myth of Iowa was firmly planted in my mind.

My nearly two years there made it the longest stretch I lived in one location. While we were poorer than landfill mice, and the men consumed a lot of alcohol, it was the only place other than the Balls that felt like home. I felt safe, and I felt loved.

We lived in a poorer section of Sioux City, east of the railroad tracks, but it was a great place to be a kid. While there I learned to ride a bike and halfway learned to ice skate. I was free to roam, explore, and build forts in the woods to my heart's content, although there was the time Grandma Brown found me in my makeshift fort after yelling several times for me to come home because it was getting dark. She chased me all the way home, threatening to "spank my hind end" if I ever scared her like that again. I got the message and would take off running to the house the instant I heard her call for me.

I don't think, though, I ever got a spanking while I lived there. When I asked Aunt Moe once if she or Grandma Brown ever spanked me, she said they never needed to. That seems strange, but I don't doubt her. I was one of those children who so badly wanted to please the adults in my life that I rarely got into trouble. That amenable personality served me well with people like the Browns and Balls. It wasn't so helpful with people like my mother and some of her dubious companions. A compliant child in a vulnerable situation is an easy target for abuse and exploitation.

Human predators are like their wild animal counterparts. They look for signs of weakness in their victims. Two things are fairly common among the children they prey upon: the absence of engaged and caring parents, and a submissive personality.

At the Browns' home I would play carefree for hours in the dirt with an odd assortment of little metal cars. A good sturdy stick would take me on many imaginary adventures. Kelly Park was like Disneyland to me with swings, slides, an awesome merry-go-round, and plenty of open space for childhood amusement. It was one of my favorite places to play. To this day, I still occasionally have dreams about it. I'm either riding my bike or climbing a tree.

Winters were magical. I would play in the snow and go sledding with my friends until I was almost frozen solid. Aunt Moe would bring me in the house, fill me with hot chocolate, dress me in dry clothes, and send me out for another round of nonstop play. My friends and I once got the snow-covered dirt path leading up to our house so slick from our sledding that the adults could hardly get up the hill. We got lectured for that, but they let us keep playing anyway.

#205. Childhood

The quality of childhood today is deteriorating, and every caring American knows something is wrong. Most kids spend three hours or more a day sitting in front of a TV, computer screen, or video game. Instead of playing creatively, they are passively watching a lot of questionable and unhealthy content.

An epidemic of obesity, depression, and the lack of critical thinking skills among our young people is the logical consequence of an "electronic childhood." What's worse — if they wanted to turn off the electronics and go outside to play, it isn't safe anymore. Many of our neighborhoods and our neighbors are no longer kid-friendly. Some are even dangerous.

Unless we find a way to make childhood possible again we will all suffer — not just the children but all of us. Let's find ways to help our children regain their childhood. Maybe the best way to start is by simply hitting the Off button.

StraightTalkwithRobertDay.org

Summers in Iowa seemed to last forever. I don't ever recall being bothered by the heat. I do remember experiencing air conditioning for the first time. Our neighbors a few houses down had installed it in their home, and my friend invited me over to see it. I thought it was way too cold. I also saw him sexually abuse his younger sister that day in his bedroom. I didn't know at the time what I was supposed to think about that. He wanted me to do it with him, even showing me what I was supposed to do. Something inside told me it was wrong, and so I left. I regret that I didn't tell anyone.

As a social worker, when I think back to the mistreatment I witnessed that day, I wonder what became of that little girl. How did that abuse affect her? I also think about my friend, how a boy my age must have learned to do that to his sister. Did he molest others? I also witnessed the same boy, on a different day, hang and beat a stray dog to death with a club. It was a gruesome and senseless act. We know now that kind of bizarre behavior can be an indication of abuse. My suspicion is that he learned his sexual aggression from an adult. Children have to be groomed to be abused and conditioned to abuse others. I do not believe that it comes naturally to them.

Growing up the way I did, with many unrelated men coming in and out of my life, made me highly susceptible for sexual abuse and exploitation. Did you know the majority of substantiated cases of child abuse are by unrelated adults in the home, usually the mother's boyfriend? Birth parents account for very few of the cases. The rate of child abuse has pretty much risen in proportion to the demise of the nuclear family. That means the best way to combat child abuse is to restore the traditional family. Imagine that.

It didn't help that my mother was so open about her sexual escapades. For my fourteenth birthday, probably motivated by the fear I might be gay because I wasn't having sex yet, she decorated my bedroom with posters of naked women. Some were pretty hard core. She gifted me, not just that day but with her overall pornographic and licentious lifestyle, with a loathsome legacy that was very difficult to shake.

I wish I could say I escaped my childhood without being victimized, but I cannot. I was abused the first time at age twelve while living with Grandma Wood. It happened at a popular swimming hole. A man who was hanging around lured me to the backseat of his car where he exposed and fondled himself. I got out of there before he did anything to me. To my surprise, many of the other boys there knew he did that kind of thing because it also had happened to them. Yet nobody reported it.

Child advocates cite statistics showing that boys are sexually abused and raped about ten percent more often than girls. For various reasons, it just isn't reported. Those who work with children should have strong policies to keep boys safe too. It's a grave mistake to think it won't happen.

There were a couple of occasions when I was a teen. Both times it happened when I was picked up while hitchhiking. The drivers showed me heterosexual and homosexual porn as a way to lower my inhibitions. I was touched and fondled a little outside my clothing, but nothing worse than that. I figured it was something I had to do in order to get where I needed to go.

I was, however, sexually abused by a church pastor when I was thirteen. After I left the Balls' home, I tried to go to church as often as I could. It meant, though, getting myself there. I went to Sunday School and Vacation Bible School a great deal during the summer months because I was drawn to the sense of security I felt there, and because I was likely to be fed.

At one particular church, the pastor took a special interest in me. I liked the attention and the treats he would buy for me. Once, while we were hiking alone together, he pulled down my pants and performed fellatio. I guess I must have been a bit stunned, because I stood there and let him do it. I also was going through puberty and was intrigued by the sensation. He then dropped his pants and wanted me to reciprocate. I felt ashamed and said no. Thankfully, he didn't insist. He tried the same thing on a couple of other occasions, but other than stroking me, nothing else happened. He eventually lost interest and started spending time with another boy. Many years later I was not surprised to learn that he had been kicked out of another church he was pastoring because of a scandal that involved several boys and young men.

None of that ever occurred in Iowa. Somehow I was safe there. But it was those kinds of things that happened to me in Tennessee and Kentucky that caused me to long so much for Iowa.

When I lived with Mom and Dad Ball, I was Robby. When I lived with Aunt Moe, I was Bobby. So was the dog. In fact, there was a succession of dogs named Bobby. When Aunt Moe got married and had children of her own, she named her first son Bobby. I guess I left a big impression on them. I know they did on me.

When I was struggling back in Appalachia, living with my Grandma Wood or in some other "gawd awful" situation, I would yearn for Iowa. It was my most common dream, day or night. Things were generally so bad there that I set Iowa up in my mind to be something much more than it actually was. It helped.

When I was a junior in high school in Tennessee, I conducted a number of money-making schemes to raise the funds to travel to Iowa. There was a 50/50 drawing that my friend was fixed to win. I broke school rules and covertly sold candy bars from my locker for five times retail. I received donations from girls after telling my sad story in a way that would create maximum emotional impact. I did pretty well, too. But my buddies who assisted me on these unethical projects convinced me to use the money instead to rent a houseboat for a weekend of fun and frolic. I did. It was a stupid and wrong thing to do all the way around.

Many years later, while speaking at a missions conference in Kansas City, I finally was reunited with my four brothers, Aunt

Moe, and Everett Brown. They were able to confirm some of my memories of what happened while we lived there in that city.

I also eventually made it back to Sioux City. I wish it had been on different terms, however. I went to perform the funeral service of my brother Joe. While there, in the city I so often longed for, I came to fully understand and appreciate the context of my Iowa dreaming.

It was quite amazing, actually. I remembered streets, buildings, and parks, even if they were no longer there. The little four-room house I lived in with Aunt Moe and four others was no longer there; however, I remembered where it stood, the layout of the yard, and much of the surrounding environment.

The notebooks full of photographs that Aunt Moe showed me finally put it all into proper perspective. The pictures showed just how cramped that house really was and how poor we really were. I know everything seems bigger and better when you're a child, but this was something else entirely. My memories confirmed the photos, and the photos confirmed my memories. I just didn't realize we were so shockingly poor.

While growing up very poor gave me a twisted worldview, there were two valuable life lessons I gleaned from my poverty. First, the negative effects of poverty on a child can be easily overcome by an abundance of affection. A nurturing-love is the antibody that counters the contagious infections of impoverishment. Second, the fewer things you want, the happier you will be in life. I'm probably tempted by materialism as much as the next person, but growing up without many belongings taught me that I can live contentedly without a lot of "stuff," as comedian and social critic George Carlin calls it.

Memories, like poverty, are relative. It's all a matter of perspective. Looking at Iowa from my difficult circumstances in the mountains of Tennessee and Kentucky showed a pretty good life. But my Iowa dreaming was just that—a dream, a myth. Love must have made the difference. The unconditional love I was shown there by Aunt Moe, Aunt Sweetheart, and Grandma Brown in those humble circumstances made it all so much bigger and better than it really was. I didn't have much when I lived there, but I was happy, and happy is enough.

They say that perception is reality. In this case, hallelujah!

What are we going to do?

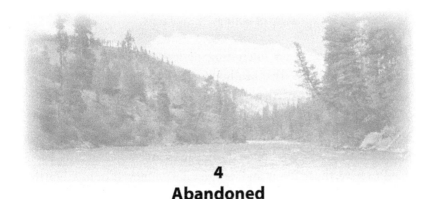

4
Abandoned

I call it "mourning the loss that never happened."

X MARKS THE SPOT. On a map, it can designate the beginning of a journey or the final destination. It can also symbolize the place where a secret is hidden (like a treasure) or when something isn't known (like a name). For me, X marks the space on my birth certificate where the name of my father should be. For many years it was hidden. When the secret was finally revealed, it proved to be no treasure.

Child's Name: Robert Jay Wood
Mother's Name: Cora Evelyn Wood
Mother's Age: 16
Mother's Occupation: Student
Father's Name: X

That means my mother either didn't know who my father was at the time this document was filed or was unwilling to acknowledge it.

In the year I was born, 1961, the circumstances of my birth represented only about three to five percent of all childbirths nationwide—"illegitimate." The numbers were much higher in Appalachia where my mother was from, but illegitimacy was fairly uncommon in the rest of the country.

"Illegitimate" is an interesting designation for a child with unknown paternity. Thankfully, long before my birth certificate was recorded, that particular word and worse words like bastard and whoreson had officially been discontinued. Edna Gladly, that great champion for children from Texas who placed over 10,000 babies with adoptive parents during her career, successfully lobbied to have those terms and designations removed from all birth and adoption records. She won her argument against the status quo when she famously proclaimed, "There are no illegitimate children, only illegitimate parents."

Today we use the term "out-of-wedlock." However, that broad designation does not capture the same thing as not knowing the identity of the child's father. Today the national average of children born out-of-wedlock hovers around 48%, and in some communities it's at an unsustainable 73%. There is incapacitating poverty, unbridled violence, and wholesale hopelessness in the neighborhoods where the majority of households are led by single parents.

So I was born at a time when the stigma of unknown paternity and unwed pregnancy was dissipating quickly, and for very good reasons; but the number of those in that "unfortunate situation" was about to explode. Those who were pregnant with, or gave birth to, illegitimate children were called "unfortunate girls" or "women of unfortunate circumstance" if the speaker was trying to be kind. They were often called much worse.

It was the beginning of the decade of the sixties and the sexual revolution that forever changed the way our society viewed these kinds of things. Birth control, feminism, and *Roe v. Wade* were just around the corner. I consider myself lucky that I was conceived prior to 1974. There is no doubt in my mind that my mother would have aborted me if that had been a viable option for her. Once, when she was really drunk, she said as much.

In the mountains of east Tennessee, however, I was just another statistic in the ongoing drama of that fallen culture. As a member of the larger society, I was part of the first wave that later became a tsunami of fatherless children. The current epidemic of fatherlessness is one of the main factors in the growing rednecking of America. If you want to know what America will look like if it stays on its current path, just look at the Appalachian region. A culture of poverty and a poverty of culture have many negative consequences, even in places and among people who aren't poor.

There are plenty of famous rednecks with money who live in ritzy Hollywood, California. Their choices and lifestyles aren't unlike many of the poor who live in Harlan, Kentucky. There is an old saying in the African-American community, "When white folks catch a cold, blacks folks get pneumonia." That is typically used in reference to the economy. When there is an economic downturn, it might cause hardships for whites but will be devastating to a majority of blacks already mired in poverty. I think it also appropriately describes what happens when the culture turns corrosive. When the wealthy and middle class get morally sick, it is the poor who die from the virus. Things like divorce, out-of-wedlock births, drug use, and delinquency have fewer negative consequences on the rich than on the poor. The poor don't have the hedge of protection that money, influence, and power affords for those with resources. A wealthy single mom will naturally be faced with some challenges, to be sure, but a poor single mom with fewer resources, trapped in a hollow or ghetto, will have battles that she most likely will not be able to overcome.

Children of affluence are generally presumed to be at low risk. However, recent studies have suggested problems in several domains — notably, substance abuse, anxiety, depression, and eating disorders. In fact, studies have shown that middle and upper class youth have higher rates of drug use than their poorer counterparts.

The first time I met my biological father was the same day I learned that the man I had thought was my father wasn't. It happened within days of my brothers' dramatic abduction. My mother suddenly announced one day that someone was coming to see me. See me? That was new. My curiosity was piqued. I asked her, "Who's coming to see me?"

"Your dad."

"But I thought you were mad at him for taking the boys."

"He is not your dad." There was strong emphasis on "He."

"Is he not my dad because you guys are divorced now?"

"No. He's not your dad because he was never your dad."

When I was back in Iowa living with Aunt Moe, two cousins (twin girls) thought they were being clever when they told me that their uncle, Everett Brown, was not my "real dad." That naturally led to a big confrontation. I was adamant that he was my dad. But then they offered two pieces of evidence that threw me for a loop. The first was a framed wedding photo that I had seen many times before but never thought anything of it. There was the groom, Everett Brown, the man I thought was my father. The bride was undoubtedly my mother. And I'm in the photo, standing between them. They tried to explain to me that the photo proved I was illegitimate. I remember that they even used the word bastard, which they thought was funny, but I wasn't getting what they meant. Frustrated by my lack of comprehension, they finally pulled out the obvious proof that apparently everyone but me understood.

"If he is your dad," they argued, "Then why aren't you living with him and your mom?"

My best response, "Because."

"Because why?"

"Just because."

When my debating skills failed to convince them, I did what all kids do when they're trapped by such airtight logic—I hit them. After the two of them let me up off the ground, I left in a huff. Because of that argument, I went for years falsely assuming that I did not live with my mother and brothers because Everett Brown didn't want a bastard living in his house. I was born before he married my mother and therefore I had no place in his family. It was only much later that I learned the truth—it was my mother who didn't want me there. It was part of her pattern that was played out all through my childhood.

Now, out of nowhere, on the front porch of my grandmother's dilapidated old house, my mother was confirming, in a rather nonchalant way, that what the twins had told me was true. Everett Brown, in fact, was not my father. The stranger coming to see me that day was my real dad.

I think it's sad that so many children today have to use all kinds of qualifying adjectives to identify the men who serve as father figures in their lives. There are the official ones: stepfathers, foster fathers, adoptive fathers, and real fathers (what is sometimes referred to as biological or birth fathers). At Patrick Henry Family Services we have "house-fathers" who selflessly help care for the children in our homes. For many kids, even those descriptors don't work. They have to get creative when speaking about their unofficial, substitute fathers. They say, "He is like my real father." Or they might introduce him with, "He's been like a father figure to me."

Don't get me wrong. I am extremely thankful for all those different types of fathers. I praise the Lord for men who are willing to stand in the gap and become fathers to the fatherless, to be a dad to those who need one. While not the ideal, it's a hundred times better than the child having no father figure at all. I am thoroughly convinced that to be a substitute father, officially or unofficially, is one the greatest acts of human kindness. The Bible calls it "pure and undefiled religion."

What do 90% of homeless and runaway children have in common with 85% of youth in prison and 75% of teens in drug treatment? You guessed it. There are no active fathers in their lives. Furthermore, did you know that fatherless children are associated with 71% of pregnant teenagers, 63% of youth suicides, and 71% of high school dropouts?

According to these statistics, fatherlessness is at the very heart of every major social problem facing children and teens today. But we don't hear much about that from the media, academia, or politicians. Why is that? Our nation's cultural elites ignore the connection between fatherlessness and these social problems because it does not fit their vested interest and narrative. They love to tout things like poverty, racism, and poor education for the ills of our youth. These social inequities require complicated and expensive solutions that only experts can address, or so they try to convince us. But in reality, much of what afflicts our children can be easily prevented by the presence of a father in the home, and if not in the home, then at least present in their lives in some tangible way. No new laws are needed. No more taxes have to be raised. No more programs need to be built and administered by government bureaucrats. All it would take to solve much of what harms our children is a dad. It's that simple.

In the end, it's not the type of dad but it's the quality of the dad that counts. It can be a step, foster, adoptive, or just a substitute or even a spiritual dad. What's important is that someone serves in the role and performs the function of a father for every child. The particular man serving in that capacity doesn't have to be the real father in order to be a real dad. In truth, he may be far superior. It's a matter of the quality of love and the quantity of time given that makes the difference.

I had all those kinds of fathers throughout my life, but few of them were the kind of dad I longed for or needed. My fathers came in this strange order: no father, foster father, stepfather, no father, real father, foster father, no father, adoptive father, stepfather, no father. I started life without a father and I live today without a dad. Every Father's Day painfully reminds me of that fact.

"What's his name?"

"Sonny Bray."

Sonny was his nickname. Billy, not William, was his given

name. To me he is simply the sperm donor, the man who got my mother pregnant. He was eight years older than her. That made him twenty-four when she got pregnant. That would have made it statutory rape at the time, and maybe that's why there's just an X on the birth certificate.

Sonny was a likeable enough guy. He was a man of few words and had a nice smile. I have his brown eyes, and I can thank him for my full head of thick hair. Because of the genes he passed on to me, I may never have to worry about baldness, but I may have to worry about cancer.

The day I first met him, he took me out for a "real" chocolate milkshake. It was the first time I can remember ever having one from a restaurant. Aunt Moe used to make homemade shakes for me when she thought I deserved a treat, but I thought it was really cool getting one from a diner. The next day he came back and took me to the store and bought me a bag of green plastic army men. What a thrill! Some of those little toy soldiers were with me all the way through high school and even college. The third day Sonny took me to a nice restaurant for dinner. I ordered pork chops. As a ten-year-old boy starved for attention, I thought those three days were the best.

Then he was gone.

I saw him on a few occasions after that. My mother and I stayed with him for part of a summer in a small broken-down old trailer. We both got scars from our time there. One night he beat her so badly she ended up at the hospital. She had permanent scars on her ears where he ripped out her earrings.

I received mine when I accidentally rode my bicycle off a wooden bridge to the rocky creek below. I got seven stitches in my chin and still have the scar to prove it. Another time I was hit by a drunk driver while riding the same bike. I was in the hospital for three or four days for head injuries. I was on my way to a Little League game where I was starting catcher. All I can remember is waking up in the hospital saying repeatedly, "I don't have on any underwear."

I also received second-degree burns and sun poisoning from playing unsupervised for too long at the public pool at Cove Lake State Park. My father didn't know I was there and my mother didn't care. I can't remember a time in my life when I was more physically miserable.

For a brief time I stayed with Sonny's sister and her family. That was one of the good places. On another occasion, I stayed with his mother for a short period. She was diabetic. I can easily remember playing with her used insulin needles. I would throw them like darts at an orange or apple. One advantage of poverty is that it forces creativity.

Equipped with nothing but my imagination, I could spend hours playing in the woods, especially in a creek. In the summers I have taken the boys at Patrick Henry on excursions to the nearest creek, where we hunt for crawdads, skip rocks, swim, and explore. At first, many of them don't know what to do but they quickly figure it out. As far as I'm concerned, children need to spend more time in unstructured play in the forests and fields than in front of an electronic screen or in a room full of toys. It is one reason Patrick Henry Family Services invested in a summer camp (Hat Creek Camp). I believe strongly that it's not just developmentally important for all kids, but therapeutically essential for children with life-challenges.

Sonny arrived one morning and cooked French toast for his mother and me. French toast was a new experience. I loved it! He showed me how to make it. Today my family loves the secret French toast recipe that I learned from him. Except for trying to tell me about sex by using graphic pornography, it was the only thing he taught me, or the only family heirloom I received from him.

I don't ever remember calling him dad, and I certainly never called him father. I unwittingly obeyed scripture throughout my life—I called no man father. On those rare occasions when he was around, I just called him Sonny.

He and I never roughhoused, never played catch, never watched a movie, never went to a ballgame or on a hike together. We never worked in the yard together, never prayed together, never did homework together, never went fishing or hunting together. We never did a thousand and one things that fathers and sons do together throughout a lifetime without ever giving a second thought about the significance of what they're doing or learning or becoming.

One summer my mother sent me to a camp for boys near the Smoky Mountains so that I could "be with other boys and learn manly things." I was sponsored by one of the beer joints where my mother was employed. I cannot recall the actual name of the camp, but for many years I have referred to it as the Schlitz Beer Camp for Wild Boys.

Apparently, boys from all over east Tennessee were sponsored by taverns that sold Schlitz Beer. It had the usual things summer camps offer: swimming, boating, archery, etc. But each night for the evening program we watched films with beer commercials. We were also given a t-shirt, hat, and towel that had Schlitz Beer plastered on them. Mine were stolen on the last day.

It wasn't fun. I did not enjoy myself. I didn't learn any of the manly arts. In fact, I didn't learn anything in the midst of the chaos of unsupervised juvenile delinquents, except that cool boys steal and fight and that real men sit around, drink beer, and pretty much do nothing. I already knew that.

To this day, I still occasionally find myself uncomfortable in the company of other men. I often get embarrassed for not knowing something that men commonly know, the kinds of things they would have talked to their dads about, the kind of stuff they would have learned from them.

#370. Not Good Enough

Children are not raised by programs, governments, or villages; they should be raised by two parents who are fervently, even irrationally, devoted to their children's well-being. Though the benefits of two parents are beyond dispute, many children — in some communities, most children — are raised by one parent.

Governments are good at transferring money but not so good at transforming people. They peddle self-esteem that never seems to translate into self-respect. They naturally stir up a sense of entitlement, while dampening the flames of personal character. They can build solid bureaucracies, but they can't build strong families. They can subsidize a family, but they've yet to find a good substitute for it.

Our goal should not be to enlarge the welfare state. The wreckage of this ill-conceived idea is strewn all around us. What was designed to be a safety net has become a trap. What was intended to support children has decimated the family, especially the role of the father. Good intentions are no longer good enough.

StraightTalkwithRobertDay.org

After he battered my mother, Sonny stayed away until I was sixteen. Then, just like the first time I met him, out of the blue my mother announced, "Someone is coming to see you." It was Sonny. We visited briefly, then he made arrangements with me to spend the next day together. He never showed up and he didn't call.

A quarter of a century later, I was officiating a wedding in a small church. The bride was getting married for the third time, the groom for his second. As I was addressing the few attendees about the sanctity of marriage, hoping something might stick this time round, I saw him. I had to look a couple of times while still concentrating on what I was saying to make sure, but it was undoubtedly Sonny. He had a patch over one eye. He had grayed quite a bit; but it was him, my real dad.

He stuck around after the service to speak with me. I invited him to my home to meet my wife and four children (his grandchildren); to my surprise he accepted. The visit was awkward. Not having much history together, the conversation lagged uncomfortably for intervals of time. He showed no interest in my family, or in what I had done in the preceding twenty-five years. He had something to tell me and eventually got around to it. Sonny explained that he had terminal cancer. It was a brain tumor directly behind his right eye. He had already lost that eye, hence the patch. He went on to say that he was moving back to the area so there would be some support for him in his last days. He didn't ask anything from me, and I didn't offer anything to him.

Perceiving that this might be my last opportunity, I did ask questions about his family and his past. I learned the name of his father and grandfather. If what he told me was true, that made him illegitimate as well. Additionally, there would have been motivation to keep his paternity a secret because of the scandalous nature of those it involved. If his claim was valid, then his grandfather, my great grandfather, was a well-known preacher in the area who was credited with starting a Pentecostal denomination. I wish I knew more, but likely never will. Yet I take solace in the thought that there may be a righteous lineage in which I belong. Perhaps I inherited not only the curse of one family tree but also the blessings of another.

Sonny also told me a little bit about meeting my mother. He said he had loved her. He also informed me about some of his other children, seven all together (eight counting me): one in Michigan, three in Georgia, and the others in Kentucky. He reminded me that I had met his Kentucky children once but my memory of that is foggy. We had a pleasant and polite visit, much like visiting with a traveling vacuum-cleaner salesman. I learned something, yet no deal was struck. I was glad I had talked to him.

Then one evening some months later, I received a phone call from an acquaintance. In fact, it took me a few seconds to figure out who it was. She told me she had news about my dad. I asked, "Which dad?" She easily could have been referring to three or four of my different dads of whom she had knowledge or with whom she had a connection. I was completely caught off guard when she said, "Your real dad." Very few people knew that Sonny Bray was my biological father. Somehow she knew, and for some reason she thought I should be made aware that he was in his last days at a nearby nursing facility.

At first I had no intention of visiting him. I didn't see the point. Then, for some reason I can't explain, I suddenly took off to see him. I found him languishing in his bed, obviously in a great deal of pain. The room was sparse. There were no flowers, no cards, nor any evidence he had had any visitors. I leaned over and spoke in his ear, "Do you know who I am?"

He nodded and then whispered, "You're my firstborn."

"Yes, that's right."

It took much effort for him to speak and I didn't have anything to say, so I awkwardly stood there wondering what to do. For some reason I just started rubbing his legs. That seemed to bring him some comfort, so I continued for a while. I asked a nurse a few questions about his status. It was not good. Then I leaned over to say goodbye.

"I guess this will be the last time we see each other."

He looked me in the eyes and said softly and slowly, "You're a real gentleman."

That is the closest thing to a father's blessing I ever got from any of my dads, official or otherwise. I thanked him and left the room.

Three days later I found myself debating whether or not to attend his funeral. This time curiosity was the primary motivator. I decided to skip the funeral but to go to the visitation the night before to see what I could learn about my genetic father.

I met some of his other children. One looked like he could be my twin. He is a pastor too. God sure does work in strange ways!

There were no mysteries revealed that night, no hidden treasure where X marked the spot.

Any emotion I have, or ever had, about my real father is the feeling of regret that I didn't have a father, not really. Any mourning I experience today is not the lamentation of losing my father, but the sorrow of never having one. If you can relate, then here's some friendly advice. Turning your back on nothing, leaving what never happened, and walking away from a relationship that never took place is not disloyal or selfish or unkind. It's self-respect and the path to healing.

People who work with children should understand something. Children growing up without a parent mourn just like those children who have lost a parent from divorce or death. The problem is that their grief is a slow-burning, unidentifiable pain. There are no events to call back to, and no moments to move forward from. It's just there, unseen and unknown, even by the child. They don't realize they're grieving but they display it in their deportment. I call it "mourning the loss that never happened." The pain of that loss can result in all kinds of unproductive and even disturbing behaviors.

Update: Just a couple of months ago while writing this book, I decided to try a subscription to Ancestry.com. I didn't have much confidence in its ability to help me plot, let alone unravel, my convoluted family tree. One night, though, while logged on trying to find clues, one of those little green leaves appeared. I followed it to a document that was the equivalent of finding X over hidden treasure. It was the marriage license of Cora Brown and Billy Bray. According to that document, the two of them had actually gotten married a few weeks after I met him for the first time. I never knew that. My mother never told me. Neither did he. But that wasn't all. A second leaf took me to their divorce papers. They were married about six months.

I take some consolation that at least for a short time, ten years after my birth, my real dad was my actual dad. I just wish I had known it at the time, because for at least those six months, I could say that I was not an illegitimate bastard.

When I consider the broken relationship of my parents, Cora and Sonny, and the many sinful choices they made, I see a biblical truth that echoes throughout the scriptures: we are not punished for our sins, we are punished by them. Yet to God's glory, and to our great benefit, with every sin comes a seed of grace hidden within it. I just wish they both could have seen that I was that seed of grace. I would have given anything then for them to know what I know now; that raising a child right, that making the sacrifice to properly love and care for him, is a deeply rewarding life. It is more than enough. They didn't need whatever it was they were searching for with all their reckless, self-absorbed consumption. Grace, in the form of a child, was graciously given to them and they rejected and abandoned that remarkable gift.

What are we going to do?

5
Bullied

I was the hillbilly from Tennessee. For that reason alone,
I was bullied without mercy.

DESPITE THE THEME SONG of the mega-hit show *The Beverly Hillbillies*, California was not the place I wanted to be. In fact, the long-running popularity of that silly sitcom may have been a factor in the nightmare that was my brief time there.

Sometime after I was taken from the basement of the tavern to live with Grandma Wood, my mother hooked up with Eddie Hill. He was some sort of police officer, and at first I had great hopes for him. In the end, though, he too became another in a series of my mother's follies. More accurately, she turned out to be one his follies.

For some reason known only to them, he and my mother headed out to southern California. Meanwhile, I wasted away in the custody of Grandma Wood, who was a true hillbilly in the classical, historical meaning of the term. But living with her was no comedy.

Like my own mother, Grandma Wood moved often. I stayed with her on and off in a number of deplorable places but normally not for very long. This time was different. This time it seemed that I was there to stay. I'm not sure what agreement she had with my mother, but I have little doubt that Grandma Wood "drew" on me. She would have gotten an extra portion on her welfare, but she was probably getting another subsidy as well. I believe I was in Kinship

Care, a type of foster care. If that was the case, then she was also getting money from Social Services.

People on welfare or disability in that part of the country often refer to it as "taking a draw." One young teacher from the north was once stumped when she asked her southern student what her mother did for a living. The girl said that her mother drew. The teacher thought she meant her mother was an artist. No, the child meant that her mother received a regular check from the government.

I went with Grandma Wood on a couple of occasions to the welfare office. She would chide me to pay close attention because I would have to draw myself one day. There also were times I stood in line with her, or for her, to receive an allotment of government handouts like cheese, potatoes, and beans. It didn't matter if we needed or even used the food. If it was being given away free, we were going to get some.

At this particular time she was living in an old two-story farmhouse on about an acre of land. It was actually one of the better places she lived. There were chickens and, at times, pigs. Grandma Wood knew how to make some good fried chicken. She would go out to the chicken pen, catch a hen, wring its neck, chop off its head, boil it, pluck it, gut it, fry it in about a half an inch of lard, then serve it with some cooked poke salad we had picked the same day. Now that's fresh chicken.

The house had rudimentary electrical wiring in some, but not all, of the rooms. There was no plumbing. We hauled water from the Bears Den, which was a pipe coming out of granite rock on the side of a mountain on highway 25W, about fifteen miles from the house. It was the best water by far. We would fill up about eighty to a hundred one-gallon used milk jugs and haul them back to the house in her beaten-up station wagon. We used that water to drink, cook, and bathe (which wasn't often).

The bathroom facility was an outhouse about forty yards from the back porch. And yes, we used old newspapers and magazines to wipe ourselves. To be truthful, we didn't use the outhouse that often. If it was cold, or hot, or dark, or raining, or sunny, or we were just too lazy to make the trip to that smelly wooden box, we just went off the back porch. I understand that is disgusting, but I'm just telling you how we lived.

Since doing laundry was a chore that required hauling a lot of water, we didn't do it that often. We didn't have to. There were a couple of charitable clothes closets happy to provide used clothing and other items to the poor like us. We had one room in the house designated for all the clothes we collected. When it was time to change our clothes (which was entirely up to each of us), we just rummaged through that enormous mound until we found something that fit. We would throw our old worn-out garments in the garbage pile over the side of a hill by the house. Almost every country road in eastern Kentucky back then had those unsightly roadside trash dumps. All of our garbage went there.

The strange thing is that we went to the county dump at least once a week, not to take trash but to get some. Grandma Wood was a scavenger. There seemed to be nothing she enjoyed more than picking through the garbage for some kind of treasure: shoes, knickknacks, tools, toys, food, you name it. If she thought she could use it or sell it at a flea market, she would rescue it from the dump. We used to joke among ourselves that Grandma Wood would spend a dollar to make a dime. It was cash money she didn't have to claim for welfare.

One winter day, I can remember my hands getting so cold from picking through the trash that I began to complain. After ignoring my many pleas for awhile, she finally got tired of it and submerged my hands in a mud puddle and held them there until I stopped crying.

Many times on the way to or from the landfill, or just about any time we were going to town, we would walk along the road with empty buckets and collect the pieces of coal that had fallen off the coal trucks. The bigger the pieces, the better—larger pieces would fill our buckets sooner and we could get on to town.

That's how we stayed warm during the winter. There was one coal stove attached to the fireplace in the center of the house. Needless to say, there were some winter nights when I thought I was going to freeze to death. On those bitterly cold nights, I would crawl into the middle of the giant pile of used clothes to stay warm.

Other than myself and Grandma, there were five of her children staying there: three uncles and one aunt. One of my aunts had recently married and moved out at the tender age of thirteen. The remaining aunt was two years younger than me, the child of my grandmother's current boyfriend and thus the favored one. He didn't live there because that would have negatively affected the draw, but he was there nearly every day and nobody messed with his daughter.

So that left me at the bottom of the pecking order, a pretty rough place to be. The unpleasant tasks nobody else wanted to do were delegated to me. Tasks like going outside no matter what the weather was like and moving the antenna so we could watch reruns of *The Andy Griffith Show*; fetching food from the kitchen whenever somebody wanted something to eat; waiting in line behind everyone else to get supper; bringing Grandma Wood her false teeth from wherever she had left them; and worst of all, emptying Grandma's five gallon excrement bucket she used in her room and discarding the piles of ripped sheets she used as feminine napkins.

Being the "boarder" in the house, I was also an easy target for bullying and theft. Mom and Dad Ball would send me gifts that would disappear rather quickly. My relatives took them or my grandmother sold them at the flea market. If I demanded my rights, I was shown the ground as proof that I was wrong.

I was named after my uncle Robert, who was only two years older. He and I slept in an attic bedroom that looked like something from a horror movie. The previous occupant had drawn dozens of scenes of death and mutilation on the walls and ceiling. They included watercolor and pencil renderings of various ways a person can kill himself and others: guns, knives, ropes, impalement, beheading; you get the picture. It was rumored that the person who drew (proper use of the word) these morbid works of art committed suicide in that very room. I don't know if it's true, but it certainly was a freaky place to fall asleep.

One evening on my way to bed, I opened the door and began to go upstairs when I stopped dead in my tracks. I was horrified as I watched the body of a boy tumbling down the stairs. I jumped back and screamed. Everyone came over to see what had happened but began teasing me for my wild imagination. But I know what I saw. I do not believe in ghosts, but I do believe in evil spirits, and something occupied that ghoulish room. Years later my uncle Robert was hit by a train and killed after drinking too much. It was eerily similar to one of the scenes of death depicted in the attic space we shared together.

The saddest part about living there was the lack of joy. There were no games, no fun, no singing. There was a makeshift basketball hoop on a power pole in the front yard, but that was the scene of more fights than good times. Occasionally we watched television together, but it wasn't a group event. For the most part, we kept to ourselves and avoided each other as much as possible. We were a house of lonely individuals looking out for ourselves. We were not a family. Love was not part of that house.

My thirteenth birthday was a particularly bad day. My mother came and brought me a telescope—not fancy or expensive but really cool, I thought, and an especially thoughtful gift. I should have known she was setting me up for a fall. After I opened my present, she announced that she and Eddie Hill were moving to California and I would continue living with Grandma Wood. Being a compliant child, I did not openly display my hurt and anger. Instead, I quietly went to my room, packed a bag full of things, and made plans to run away. I thought to myself, "There is no way I am living here any longer." Up to that moment, I believed that staying was temporary as before, but the idea of living there for good was more than I could take.

My spoiled young aunt informed on me. My mother came into my room and demanded to know what I was doing. I said I was running away. I told her I was sick of living there and tired of all her crap. I finally rebelled! She lost it.

My mother had a very low tolerance for any word or action she deemed unappreciative. I remember one Christmas I had asked for a guitar. I didn't expect a real one but something I could pretend to play. A couple of days before Christmas my mother wanted me to guess what she had gotten me. I held the package, shook it a little bit, and then told her I thought it was a guitar. She instantly got moody and stopped talking for the rest of the day. The next morning that gift was missing from under the tree. She had returned it. I got nothing from her that year. That was her way of punishing me. She wanted it to be a surprise and my accurate guess took that away from her.

Another time I spoiled her fanciful illusions that she was the perfect mother. It happened while I was sitting in the back seat of a car on the way back to my hillbilly prison. My mother had picked me up at Grandma Wood's in the morning with the promise of spending the day together, which included getting a chocolate milkshake. That never happened. Instead I waited all day in her sparsely furnished apartment with no TV, while she had sex with a man with a disfigured face that I didn't know. When they finally exited the bedroom, they decided he would drive us back to my grandmother's house. When he stopped for gas, I asked my mother when she was going to buy me the milkshake she had promised. "Not this trip," she told me. Then I reminded her that she had also promised to spend the day with me and not screwing some ugly stranger. She whirled back in her seat up front with a look like she could kill me. She smacked me hard several times. In a whispering scream she told me to stop crying and acting like a baby before her "friend" got back in the car, or I would live to regret it.

With this history of emotional instability, my mother blew a mental gasket that morning of my thirteenth birthday. She saw my running away as the ultimate act of disrespect and selfishness. She was proud of herself for buying me such a nice present and oblivious to my pain at yet another rejection. She would teach me to show appreciation!

She started screaming profanities at me, but before I could get two words out in defense, she picked up my birthday gift and started striking me with it as hard as she could. I tried to duck and cover, but she just kept beating away at me, indiscriminately hitting me wherever she could. I had received a lot of whippings from her over the years, but this was by far the worst beating I ever got. She stopped when the telescope was so shattered that there was nothing left for her to wield. She then punched with her fists and kicked with her feet. After what seemed like an eternity, she stomped out of the room and left for California without saying goodbye. I cried myself to sleep. My grandmother kept me home from school the next couple of days. You don't have to explain bruises and black eyes that way.

My dreary existence at the Wood estate carried on as before, but now with an intense sense of hopelessness. School was my only refuge. I enjoyed going, even though I was not a good student. I never did homework. No one at home ever asked or expected it. But neither did my teachers—"the soft bigotry of low expectation" as George W. Bush would call it.

Only two out of the eleven of my mother's siblings graduated from high school: Thomas and Hiram, two uncles I admired for playing sports, working at a real job, taking regular baths, and having "town friends." Education just wasn't valued in the Wood family. In fact, my mother would often accuse me of "putting on airs" or "acting above my raising" if I showed any interest in learning. That is one way poor people keep other people poor. It's peer pressure to stay in the gutter. Because if you get out, that says more about them than it does you.

I got along well with all my teachers and that was how I made it through my childhood and adolescence. I had little trouble getting other adults to accept and like me. It was my own family who couldn't or wouldn't. I was another mouth to feed, but I was also another monthly check to draw. I was like the dog some people keep chained to a tree in their backyard and you wonder why they even have a dog. Minimum care is provided but no love is shown. It serves some purpose to the owner but the poor dog rarely, if ever, knows it. True dog lovers observe it with confusion and compassion but cannot do much. After all, it isn't their animal.

Then the day came when Grandma Wood announced that I was moving to California to be with my mother. I'm not certain what happened to change the plan or if this had always been the plan. If I was in Kinship Care, then Social Services allowed me to return to my mother who now had a job and a home in California. Needless to say, I was pleased to hear the news.

Eddie Hill drove from Ontario, California, a suburb of Los Angeles, to Jellico to get me. It took us four days of hard driving in his Volkswagen Beetle to get back. The days on the road were long and boring, but I got to see a lot of the country. While passing through Texas, I ate my first burrito. He was surprised I didn't know anything about Mexican food. He was surprised I didn't know about a lot of things. He knew, though, that I loved chocolate milkshakes and made sure I got one each day of our marathon cross-country journey.

I liked Mr. Hill. Unlike many of the other men my mother brought around, he seemed to take genuine interest in me. He never made me a promise he didn't keep. Spending time with just him on that road trip was mostly enjoyable.

However, things seemed to change as we got closer to our destination. He made more stops than we had earlier and he used a payphone. He said he was giving my mother updates as to where we were, yet he grew increasingly agitated with each stop. He started speaking about their troubled relationship, but I didn't understand what he was trying tell me.

Not long after we crossed the California border we had an accident. Eddie Hill told the Highway Patrol that a gust of wind had flipped the car. But I didn't think so. I distinctly remember him pulling up hard and fast on the emergency brake while dramatically turning the steering wheel in one direction. The car tumbled down the freeway and spun around upside down a few times before coming to a stop. The roof was crushed and there was shattered glass all around us, but neither one of us was hurt.

A number of vehicles stopped to check on us before the troopers arrived. When everything was cleaned up, an older couple traveling in an RV took me to my mother. I never saw Eddie Hill after that. Later, my mother told me she had broken up with him. I think she must have told him during one of those phone calls. I have always thought he purposely caused the accident to get back at her but that is only speculation.

It was an interesting coincidence that I arrived at my California home in an RV. My mother's new job was at a Recreational Vehicle superstore. She lived on the grounds as well, in a modest home provided by the owners. It stood on a major highway very close to the airport; nevertheless, it was the nicest place we ever lived in together. I even made a little bit of money doing a few chores before catching the school bus in the morning and again immediately after school.

The house, the job, and even the weather were wonderful. The owners took me to Disneyland, Grauman's Chinese Theatre, and other tourist attractions. I saw an ocean for the first time. There were many delightful aspects to my time there except one—school.

I was the hillbilly from Tennessee and for that reason alone, I was bullied without mercy.

Southern California was a great deal more diverse than I had experienced in Iowa or in the mountains of Tennessee and Kentucky. Up to that time I had little contact with Blacks (the common term then) and I had never met a Hispanic. I didn't know how to relate to them or even to the other whites at the school. I was a cultural misfit. To them I was nothing more than all the worse things they thought a backwoods redneck was supposed to be. I guess in many ways I was. At first the black kids bullied me relentlessly. Then the Hispanic kids would take turns beating the snot out of me. Even the white kids picked on me with extreme prejudice and vile pleasure. The girls were also very hateful. A pack of them held me down once and stole my shoes. I got in trouble at home for that.

I tried to avoid trouble by staying in my classroom during recess, but that didn't always work. The bus ride to and from school was a daily gauntlet of harassment. I was spat on, slapped, cursed at, or robbed nearly every day. There were trips to the principal's office for mediation. Teachers tried to keep me within sight. I told my mother countless times about the intimidation and bullying at school, but she would tell me it was just something I had to learn to deal with because there would always be bullies.

There is a big difference between getting picked on and the type of bullying taking place in our schools and online today. No child should have to experience that for one single day. I find it interesting that bullying and school violence have only gotten worse the more the schools focus on the problem. You would think they would understand the principle at work here: what is focused on expands. When educators changed their attention from educating children to fixing social problems, we began getting progressively dumber students and even more social problems.

It's been my experience that bullies love weakness. They always give into the temptation of it. Evil is like that. It doesn't matter if it originates from powerful spiritual forces, from the darkness of self-centered politics, or from the juvenile mentality of mean kids on playgrounds or computers — if there is weakness it will be exploited. Even so, sometimes evil just shows up, no matter what we do or how strong we are. Oppressors will oppress. Tyrants will torment. When they do, remember this truth I wish I had known in my childhood. What happens to us does not say anything about us, but how we respond does. It's been said that life is 10% of what happens to us and 90% of how we react to it. The rotten things that happen to us do not diminish our worth or value. Our identity should never be tied to our victimization. No matter what intimidation we suffer, or the persecution we receive, we are still precious souls, loved by God, with gifts to give to the world. We should never doubt that. Ever.

#11. Safe Haven

There have always been bullies in schools and neighborhoods, but now there's a new medium for harassment and a new level of harm. The cyber bully can now reach into his or her victim's home and cause all kinds of mental and emotional injury. It's not just the new form of bullying that's unsettling but the level of viciousness now associated with it. Some have committed suicide to escape their tormentors.

The knockout game where gang members earn points by hitting innocent victims is the latest manifestation of a growing culture of violence. I don't have to explain why this is extremely troubling.

Children need to be safe from bullies and gangs. They must feel secure physically and emotionally in order to grow and mature normally. This is our first and foremost concern at Patrick Henry Family Services and is one of the main purposes of our ministry. We can provide a safe haven away from harm. Please, let us know if we can help.

StraightTalkwithRobertDay.org

I wasn't sure what was worse, living with Grandma Wood in Appalachia or going to school in California. The situation had been completely switched. For the first time in my life, home was good but school was not. But as always in my childhood, nothing lasted very long.

My mother eventually lost her job and we moved in with a guy who claimed to be a hairstylist to the stars. He shaved my mother's head because he convinced her she could be a model, and for some reason I've never understood, models had bald heads. We lived with that idiot for about two weeks before he kicked us out.

From there we "couch surfed" at a half-dozen or so odd places and with many strange people I did not know and did not like. I got a crash course on the 70s pop culture in southern California. It was nothing at all like Tennessee or Iowa. Though hippies and hillbillies share a lot more in common than you might think, it seemed to me as if I were living in a foreign country. The food, language, dress, and funny-smelling cigarettes were all unfamiliar to me. Someone took me to see the movie *Jesus Christ Superstar*. Someone else gave me a peace sign necklace. I didn't much like any of it, but I went along to get along so that I could eventually move along. What else could I do?

Finally my mother burned all her bridges. She ran out of places to stay or people who would take us into their home. She borrowed some money from somewhere and bought two Greyhound bus tickets to Tennessee. We left the nightmare of The Hotel California behind us.

Do you know how many stops a bus makes between California and Tennessee? I had one *Mad Magazine* to occupy my time. I almost went mad from the boredom.

Back in our home state she dumped me, again, with Grandma Wood. In fairly short order, all the cool clothes I got in California were gone. At school things were good again. I amazed my friends with tales of California and a new game I learned there—Wall Ball. At least I got something positive out of that awful experience. But home was the nightmare once again.

What are we going to do?

6
Exploited

It was the bone-deep, empty-soul, numb-minded
kind of hopeless exhaustion and I didn't give a
flyin-flip about what happened next.

I WAS ADOPTED WHEN I WAS SIXTEEN. That single, legal act was the beginning of the end. My mother and I were living in a two-story trailer when she met my adoptive father, Charles Day. Everyone just called him Pete.

I had never seen a two-story mobile home before, nor have I seen one since. I lived in many trailers of various sizes, models, and conditions over the years, but I had a peculiar feeling of pride living in that one-of-a-kind engineering marvel. I also lived in some interesting places with colorful names like Stinking Creek, Hoot Owl Hollow, and Frog Level, where our house was so crooked from being flooded so often that I could race my Hot Wheel Cars down the living room floor. Now I lived in a town, on a paved street instead of a gravel road. I consider Williamsburg, Kentucky, my second hometown.

Yet, as I mentioned before, living with my mother alone was never a good situation. A high volume of men came in and out of that particular locale, along with a good deal of partying that, more often than not, lasted all night. It was hard for me to stay awake at school the next day or to focus on homework, which I now was interested in doing.

In the morning, I would step over inebriated and wasted individuals on my way to the kitchen, turn off the blaring music (those were the days of eight-track tapes that could repeat endlessly), and try to find something for breakfast. If I made noise and woke up my mother, she would mumble some nasty remark. I would just ignore it and head off to school. I was in the eighth grade by then, and I knew enough to know I didn't want to be poor the rest of my life. School was starting to become something more than just a place of refuge.

To get to school, I had to walk right through the campus and across the iconic viaduct of Cumberland College. I would sometimes hang out in the Student Center after school or on the weekend to get away from my mother. Seeing and occasionally interacting with the students there undoubtedly played a role in the process of my yearning for more in life.

As providence would have it and against all the odds, that's where I would attend college five years later. It was in college that I became my own man, broke the chains of poverty, and met and married my beautiful wife. It was also in college that I started the process of healing. As providence would also have it, I returned fifteen years later to teach Social Work.

When there weren't parties in our redneck manor, I was often on my own. Because I was older and able to take care of myself, I think my mother thought that I would not be much of a bother to her lifestyle. And for the most part I was happy when left alone. I still prefer solitude to a room full of people. There was a period of four days, though, when I returned from school to an empty trailer. I wasn't sure what I was going to do if she didn't come back. I didn't know where she was, but I had a pretty good idea of what she was doing.

I can remember that so well because there was almost no food: less than half a loaf of stale white bread, two single slices of individually-wrapped cheese, a nearly empty container of mayo, and a few raw radishes someone had given us from their garden. The first day I made two cheese sandwiches for supper. The second day

I made two radish sandwiches with the last of the mayo. The third day I ate the last three slices of bread dry. It was my make-believe sandwich. The fourth day I went without supper, not even a make-believe sandwich.

Every morning I went without breakfast. My only meal was the lunch served by the school. On the fifth day I came home and found my mother there, along with some groceries. She acted like everything was normal, as if she hadn't been gone, and I behaved like everything was just fine, as if she had never left.

There was a predictable pattern when it came to food, whether I was living with Grandma Wood, my mother, or someone else on welfare. We would eat like royalty the first two weeks of the month, with Little Debbie Snack Cakes (still my favorite), Vienna sausages, Twinkies, various kinds of sugary cereal, and just about any other processed, packaged food we saw advertised on television. The last two weeks, however, were rather sparse, with a lot of pinto beans (we called them soup beans), cornbread, oatmeal, and vegetables from the garden when in season.

It was either feast or famine. Sometimes on the last few days it would be questionable whether we would have anything at all to eat. I remember more than once, while living with Grandma Wood, we raided other people's gardens in the middle of the night in order to have something to eat the next day. When the "draw" came in, we would go to the store and stock up on all the unhealthy foods we missed during the lean time. Of course, that kind of behavior only ensured that the lean days would return. It was a vicious cycle. You certainly wouldn't have wanted to be the postal worker on the first of the month and not have our check in hand.

To this very day I find myself unnecessarily worried about when I will be eating next, where I will be eating, and what I will be eating. I do not feel secure unless my pantry is well-stocked. When they first come to the Patrick Henry Boys and Girls Homes, many of the children will hide and hoard food until they know there will always be something to eat. We don't make a fuss about it. In fact, we make the pantry a focal point of their tour when they first arrive. We want them to be assured there will always be plenty to eat.

I cannot remember when or how I first met Pete Day. I do recall that my mother met him in a bar. I think it was either the Hilltop, Ponderosa, Wagon Wheel, The Spot, or the D&M (commonly referred to as the Devil's Mansion). Although none of them would have been an unusual place for her to meet men, it was the way she spoke about him that was different. She was in love. It wasn't long before they were married and we moved out of our two-story playgirl mansion. I was fifteen and in the ninth grade.

I had just turned sixteen — we were living at the foot of Kensee Hollow — when my mother and Pete Day asked if I wanted to be adopted, to officially take on his last name. I agreed. Somebody was willing to claim me and that felt good. I remember how the judge explained it to me. "When Mr. Day adopts you," he told me, "he will be your real father and no one can say that he isn't."

With a simple signature, I went from Robert Wood to Robert Day, and because my middle name rhymed with my new last name I started emphasizing it: Robert Jay Day. "Don't forget the Jay," I would tell everyone, "It's a third of my whole name."

There are two things in the adoption papers I have always found interesting. First, they identify my biological father as Billy Bray. Although he is not listed as the father on my birth certificate, he appears on the adoption record and it says that the court finds he abandoned me.

Second is this statement: "…That said child Robert Jay Day shall hereafter have all the rights and privileges of a natural born child of Petitioner including the right to inherit from him according to the laws of descent and distribution. Petitioner will pay the cost.…"

There is no clearer example of our adoptions as sons and daughters of God, our Heavenly Father. We, who are his children by faith, have all the rights of his own Son Jesus, who actually paid the price for our adoption with his own life. Isn't that amazing? I am so pleased to see the spirit of adoption taking hold in some of our churches. Our Heavenly Father has a special soft spot for the orphan. I believe he shares a portion of that love with the cosmic orphans he adopted, if they are open to it. I have seen adoption revitalize a local church.

Unfortunately, there is a counterfeit movement as well. A huge spike in the number of International and Domestic adoptions began when the government began providing subsidies as a way to encourage it. Suddenly all kinds of groups got into the business and used all kinds of tactics to get more children adopted. On the surface, this seems like a good thing. But there is a back story as well. Many of these children are not doing well and adopted families are abandoning them out of desperation. Some have been exploited for their adoption subsidies. The largest population of children we serve at Patrick Henry Family Services are children from "failed adoptions."

While Mr. and Mrs. Charles Day still enjoyed "bar hopping," we had some sense of normalcy and routine. We moved only five times in four years. I attended only two high schools. Considering I went to four different schools in the fourth grade, only two schools in four years was most agreeable to me.

But we had a secret.

The source of income that provided for my new quasi-stability was a bit dubious. Pete Day was a pot dealer. He sold cannabis from our residence (or at a bar while he was having a few drinks) and sometime pills. If it had been thirty years earlier, he probably would have been a moonshiner. Pete Day was a pioneer in the new, quickly developing mountain economy—the growth and distribution of marijuana. Now the mountain region is awash in hard drugs like Meth, OxyContin, and Heroin. These drugs are ravaging the population, depleting limited resources, and causing immeasurable harm to children.

My adoptive father often said it was "easy money." But you know the saying, "easy come, easy go." We never seemed to get ahead. Of course, any business that smokes up half of its inventory is going to struggle to make a profit. Hardly a day went by without someone, or a number of someones, sitting around our place, smoking and drinking. It's just part of the pot-smoking culture. It also doesn't help that you have to stay one step ahead of the law in order to stay in business.

On one occasion we were raided by the state police. It happened one summer afternoon when we were just hanging around our highly-financed, used, singlewide mobile home. The phone rang and I answered it. On the other end of the line was a relative who happened to work for the local police department. He said to me in a hushed tone, "Tell Pete they're coming and he better get out quick." Click. I told my legal-real-dad what I had just heard. He told my mother to hurry up, get a few items, and get in the car. He quickly gathered up his entire stash, handed it to me, and told me to run into the woods and hide it.

I have always thought it ironic that the only man in my mother's long line of men who was decent enough to legally give me his last name, and provided enough stability and provisions for a halfway normal life, was someone who made a living breaking the law. I am happy to report that Pete Day stopped those activities long ago and is a good citizen today.

I took the garbage bag half full of pot and paraphernalia, ex-ited out the back door, and ran into the woods. At that time we lived on the side of a mountain, so to go into the woods meant either going further up the mountainside or down it. Since law enforcement would be coming from below, I went up about two hundred yards of steep incline where I found a safe place to hide the evidence. I made sure it was on someone else's property just in case it was discovered. Then I went to a spot where I could see our trailer down below.

I was very familiar with that area. We got our water from a creek that ran down the mountain. We had dammed it and secretly run a system of pipes across our neighbor's property to our trailer. It was a gravity-fed system that worked about fifty percent of the time, and when it did it was often filled with silt, but we were nevertheless proud of our ingenuity. The septic system, on the other hand, was an unfinished hole in the ground with a drain field that didn't work properly. Sewage oozed to the top and formed what looked like a swamp of human waste. We were reminded of that fact on any day the wind blew from that direction towards the trailer.

From my vantage point on the mountainside, I could see that the police were already there. The place was overrun by cops. I squatted down and watched for about an hour as they went in and out of the trailer and searched the grounds around it. I could also see that my drug-dealing parents were gone. They made it out before the law arrived. Fortunately for them, the police were also raiding the suppliers who lived nearby. Pete Day drove right past the police just as they were putting his key supplier in handcuffs, his terrified wife and small children watching from inside their getaway car.

For the rest of the summer I was on my own. My parents were "on the lam." Later I learned that they camped at various places deep in the woodland with some others in the local pot syndicate. They remained there until the heat died down. I had my driver's license, a car, and a job at Kentucky Fried Chicken, so I didn't go hungry. You may interpret that second part any way you want. It will be correct. Other than an occasional bout of loneliness in the evening, I enjoyed the long break from them and our risky commerce. Buyers still came to the trailer looking to score a "dime bag," but I would either pretend I wasn't home or tell them to go away.

Pete Day never forced or pressured me in any way to participate in his illegal affairs. I am very grateful for that. There were times, however, that I sold product to someone I knew when he or my mother were not present. I was keenly aware that our livelihood depended on it, and since I often needed or wanted something for school or my growing social life, I occasionally disposed of some of the illegal merchandise.

Many of you might find this hard to believe, but I have never been drunk or high. It was freely available, and I was strongly encouraged to try it, but I have never had the slightest interest in pot. I haven't even smoked a cigarette, although practically every adult in my life has. My mother didn't smoke until she married Pete Day. It was one of the few things I admired about her. He attempted to get her off painkillers by getting her hooked on tobacco instead, but it just became one more addiction and one more unnecessary expense.

I have tasted liquor and I have had a few celebratory beers with my football buddies, but I have never been intoxicated. I'm not sure if it was the prayers of the Balls that kept me from these particular dangers or if it was my own special form of rebellion, but I never had a desire to do any of the things I saw my caretakers do on a regular basis.

That is not to say I didn't do bad things in my childhood or that I didn't have a sin issue. I most certainly did. I cheated on tests, lied often, feasted on pornography, and took things that were not mine. I learned my lessons about stealing, however, rather early.

One lazy summer day, I was running around with a friend from my fifth-grade class. He had a brand new squirt gun. I did not. We both agreed that I needed one in order to keep our imaginary adventures going. Neither of us had the capital to purchase the coveted item. My friend had a great idea. No, not to shoplift it, but rather to earn the money to buy it. We decided we would redeem pop bottles. Back then you could get five cents for an empty glass soda bottle. That was pretty good money for two young boys looking for $2.99 plus tax. The problem was we couldn't find any bottles.

Finally, my friend had another brilliant idea. Behind the Piggly Wiggly were all the bottles we could ever need. We walked to the back, picked up a six-pack in each hand, walked around to the front of the store, went inside and redeemed those bottles. In other words, we stole those bottles and then doubled our crime by selling them to the rightful owners. For some reason we did not equate that as the same thing as stealing the squirt gun.

After the first trip we didn't have enough money and we still didn't have enough after the second. We figured one more time would do it, but since the cashier had asked us where we were getting all these bottles so quickly, we knew we had better not push our luck.

On our last planned robbery of the Piggly Wiggly, the unimaginable happened. We both did as we had done before. We each grabbed a six-pack of empty bottles in each hand, but this time as we lifted them up off the ground, the bottoms of the cardboard containers gave way and the bottles crashed onto the pavement below. Maybe one reason they are called pop bottles is because of the sound they make when they break: pop, pop, pop.

My friend immediately took off running. He never even looked back. I immediately bent down and started cleaning up the mess. Stupid, right? But before I knew it, the big hairy arm of the butcher grabbed me by the back of my shirt and marched me into the manager's office. "So you are the one stealing my pop bottles." I said, "Yes sir." I did not tell on my friend. I kept the criminal code of honor: do not rat on another criminal (unless there is something to be gained by it).

The manager called the police. An officer arrived, put me in his squad car, and drove me to the city jail. He judiciously led me to an empty cell, placed me inside, and then slammed the door. That is a unique sound that I hope never to hear again. I started sobbing. He left me in there for about five minutes, maybe less, but it was long enough for me to learn the valuable lesson he was trying to convey. That was good, common-sense intervention, for which he probably would be fired and/or sued today.

He unlocked the door, came inside the cell, and asked why I stole those bottles. I told him I wanted to buy a squirt gun. He put me back in the squad car and drove me to the general store on Main Street and asked me to show him the item I wanted. I pointed it out to him. He took it off the shelf, walked me to the counter, and purchased it with his own money. He handed it to me and said, "Son, next time you need or want something, just ask someone for help. Don't ever steal again."

"Yes, sir," was my humble reply. That cop demonstrated true kindness and illustrated the beauty of grace to me that day. I shall never forget it.

I wish I could say I didn't steal anything ever again, but I cannot. It wasn't until I had a personal relationship with the One who, by an act of ultimate grace, died between two thieves for my sins that I developed the proper conscience not to take things that didn't belong to me.

#143. Do Over

Allow me to ask a straight question today. Are you happy with your life? Did you wake up today realizing that you are not where you want to be, or doing what you want to do? Have you come to the conclusion you are not the person you wanted to be when you were younger? You really don't like what you have become.

Friends, I am here to tell you today that you can change. You are not obligated to stick with the first version of your life. You can have a "do over." It's not too late. It's never too late to change.

If you have discovered that you have taken the wrong road in life, it is not too late to alter your course, to get back on track. But you must have the resolve and the courage. It won't be easy undoing some of your decisions. Some may never be undone. But, with true repentance and enough time, those bad decisions can seem like ancient memories of another person's life.

StraightTalkwithRobertDay.org

After things settled down, my parents returned from their hideout to resume business as usual. We eventually moved from there to a drafty old house. It had zero insulation and was heated only by two small fireplaces. The winter we spent there was one of the coldest and snowiest in decades. I missed four straight weeks of school. It was such a bitter winter that a cover of *Time Magazine* was titled, *How to Survive the Coming Ice Age*. We literally plundered the boards and timbers from a barn near the house to fuel the fires when we didn't have enough money to buy a car trunk load of coal.

I was miserable, not just from the cold and the constant enormous effort it took to keep the fires going, but because I felt trapped inside, in very close quarters with two people whose relationship was beginning to show strain. I began to deeply disdain them.

I also was miserable because we had sulfur water that stunk like rotten eggs, which sorely aggravated my already out-of-control acne. I developed huge boils all over my face while there. Pete Day had a remedy for that. He arranged for me to see a local physician to ask if he would give me (not prescribe) antibiotics. I kind of knew how it worked from hearing stories that he and his drug buddies told. I wasn't thrilled about it, but I was desperate to do something about my acne.

It was arranged for me to visit the doctor at his private residence after school on the same day each week. His wife, who served as his nurse at his regular office, would show me into the living room and then leave. The doctor, whom I had seen other times in his town office for all kinds of medical reasons, would ask me to drop my pants and underwear, but not take them off. He would stand, or sit, and watch. He never touched me but would ask me to get an erection and even provided "inspirational materials." It didn't matter if I achieved his request; as long as I tried he was pleased. He then would give me enough antibiotic to last another week. The following week, the exploitation—someone using his power to take advantage of a vulnerable person—was repeated.

From there we moved to a brick house. I had an encounter with a copperhead in the living room of that house that I will never forget. It was the last place I would live before I graduated. If my recollection is right and my counting correct, it was my thirty-seventh place of residence. Nearly all the houses but this last one have fallen down or been demolished. The trailers have been removed or are uninhabitable. Even the apartments no longer exist. I don't know about the condition of the California places I lived in, but all the rest are gone. This points to a sad reality. The poor have very little permanency. Few things in their lives last. Worst of all, while the poor share many things in common, they don't often share a sense of community. If they do, it doesn't last long.

My last home was actually a fairly decent place to live, but life there was anything but good. Pete Day spent almost all his time, day and night, at the taverns selling pot, buying beers, and fooling around with whores. My mother became increasingly more neurotic. On top of it all, the tension and angst of my adolescence was nearing a boiling point.

I had bought a used Chevy Vega with some of my hard-earned hourly wage. The Vega was Detroit's answer to the 70s energy crisis. It was like a disposable lighter; when it ran out of gas it was best to just throw it away. The aluminum engine blocks that made them so cheap to purchase and operate also made them so expendable. That is why it is so rare to see one on the road these days. I would have to carry water in the car with me to put in the radiator every few miles so it wouldn't overheat. Oil use was almost as bad. The driver's side door was permanently jammed and I would have to either crawl through the window or enter through the passenger side. But it had an eight-track player mounted just under the radio. That almost made up for everything. It was a piece of junk, but it was my piece of junk.

One day it just stopped running, and I couldn't get it started again. Pete Day, just returning from a long hard day at the bars with a little too much to drink, took a peek at the engine. He then pulled out the .45 caliber pistol he kept on him at all times when in public (dealing strictly in cash makes you an easy target of criminals) and unloaded the magazine on my broken-down car. He then pronounced it "officially dead."

I wrote earlier that my Grandmother Wood was a violent drunk. Well, my mother was a pitiful drunk. She would get so depressed when she drank that she often became a danger to herself and others. She also was addicted to painkillers. She took BC Powder almost hourly for a headache that she claimed never went away. I think it is what eventually killed her. She became septic when the lining of her large intestines erupted.

One day my mother had taken an especially toxic mix of alcohol and painkillers. I came home late in the evening from a ball game and found the house in turmoil. There had been an ugly argument. My mother took the gun and went into the woods where she remained for hours. I knew there would be no peace in the house and that I could not go to bed until she came back. So I went to the edge of the woods and hollered for her to come back home.

She yelled back, "I've got a gun. Don't come after me."

"What are you going to do with that gun?"

"Don't worry about it, just don't come after me."

The debate went on like that for far too long. I was tired. I was tired because it was late, and I was tired because it was the same type of craziness I had dealt with my entire life. It was the bone-deep, empty soul, numb-minded kind of hopeless exhaustion and I didn't give a flyin-flip about what happened next.

"I'm coming in. Don't shoot me."

"Don't come after me, I've got a gun."

"Yes, I know. You told me."

"Well, don't come after me then."

"I'm coming in. Shoot me or shoot yourself, but I am coming in either way."

I meant every word I said. At that moment I would have been perfectly happy if she shot and killed me or if she shot and killed herself. It really didn't matter. I felt as if I was drowning, that damned river pulling me under for the last time. There just didn't seem to be any fight left in me. Yet I took a deep breath, went into the woods, took the gun away from my mother, and left her sitting in her self-pity, while I went back to the house and to bed.

A couple of nights later I was wakened from a restless sleep to find my room on fire. I yelled, "Fire, fire." But there was no response. I went into my parents' bedroom in a panic and shook them hard while yelling as loudly as I could, but they did not wake up. I ran to the kitchen and got a pan of water and threw it on the blaze. After about a half dozen trips back and forth to the kitchen, I finally got the flames out. I went back to my parents' bedroom and once again attempted to wake them up. They stirred a little but showed no interest in what I was saying. Eventually I gave up and went to sleep on the living room couch. The next morning I got up and went to school. When I returned home they were waiting and wanted to know what I did to my room. I have long believed that my mother tried to kill us all.

Not long after that episode, I was still running on empty and desperate for change. I took the pistol and put it to my temple, stared at myself in the mirror, and wondered what it would be like to pull the trigger. I imagined the great relief it would give me. Then I put it in my mouth and seriously thought about doing it. I stood there several minutes tasting the cold metal with my tongue, figuring the proper angle for maximum damage, my finger pressed firmly to the trigger but not enough to release it. Once again, I took a deep breath, put the gun down and went on surviving.

But I was done with it all. From that point on I was determined to get out of the insanity, the poverty, the crime, the substance abuse, and the hopeless madness of the whole wretched mess—whatever it took. More than anything else, though, I wanted so badly to get away from all the emotional noise. I was weary of the drama of my psychologically volatile mother and the sorry cast of characters in her life whose only life goal was to get a buzz. I had to escape…one way or another.

Children who grow up in toxic homes will develop either a fear of emotion, holding back their feelings, or a flamboyance of emotion, overreacting to everything. They will either clam up or stir up drama. In the first case, kids learn it's best to not talk, trust, or feel. It's better to be dumb and numb than to live in the center of a constant storm. In the second case, kids live in a constant state of arousal from what is, in essence, emotional pornography. They feed on it like an addiction. They love the constant storm. Neither response is healthy. Both display low emotional intelligence.

I personally understand why some young people take their own lives. Hopelessness kills. Job 6:11-13 says, "What strength do I have, that I should still hope? What prospects, that I should be patient? Do I have the strength of stone? Is my flesh bronze? Do I have any power to help myself, now that success has been driven from me?"

Teen suicide is not just a personal tragedy, it's also a national shame. The period of our lives that should be carefree and happy is becoming so increasingly downhearted for so many of our youth that they would rather die than go on living. I believe the rate at which our children take their lives is the thermometer that measures the health and wellness of a society. If so, ours is not doing so well.

"Providing hope for tomorrow" has long been a guiding theme at Patrick Henry Family Services. In fact, we named our counseling centers Hope for Tomorrow because we believe that giving someone the intangible asset of hope can make the real difference in their lives.

What are we going to do?

7
Rescued

*A person's view of the world is small
when life itself is limited.*

DURING THAT RECORD-BREAKING winter of 1977–78, I started attending Newcomb Baptist Church, a small Southern Baptist church just down the road from the drafty old house we lived in. I continued to attend when we moved to my thirty-seventh home, even though I always went alone. As I explained before, I was drawn to church for many reasons. This particular church, however, had a specific interest for me—a pretty girl.

The church had a youth minister, which was rare for a congregation of that size and in that area. He and his wife had started as college students but stayed on to continue the work. Darrell and Darlene Shirley were young and inexperienced, but they let the Lord lead their ministry. Their genuine interest in young people attracted teens like myself to the group. I started hanging around and enjoyed many good meals and sweet fellowship in their home. They provided wise counsel, timely encouragement, and lots of potato chips and homemade chili. I was hooked.

There is no way I could ever repay the Shirleys for the multitude of kindnesses they showed me then and many times since. But as they would always tell me, "Don't pay us back. Just help someone else when you can." They were doing "pay it forward" long before the movie made it popular.

The young lady who captured my fancy was a member of the church; her father served as head deacon. He was suspicious of me from the very start because of my family, and rightfully so. Although I didn't appreciate his protective attitude at the time, now that I am a father I fully understand.

In an edict he thought would solve his dilemma, he told me I could see his daughter at church anytime I wanted. For every time I attended church I could take her out on a date (which had very strict time restraints and destinations). I'm sure he thought I would not abide by those guidelines and would leave his daughter alone, or I would hear the gospel and change. Either way, it would be better than just letting me have unlimited access to her. He was a wise man.

Shortly after the rules were explained to me, the church had their annual fall revival, a week-long series of evangelistic meetings. That was my chance to bag a half-dozen future dates in one week. I had been to a lot of church services before, but I had never been to a Baptist revival like that.

Brother Joe Mobley was an evangelist from the old school. He preached hard, loud, and long. He believed in moving around when he preached—a lot. He always wore red socks no matter how he was dressed. He said it kept him grounded to the blood of Jesus that washes away the sins of the world.

I was skeptical at first. Plus, I was distracted by the young lady I was there to see. But by the end of the week I was fit to be tied. By the time of the invitational hymn on the last night, I was "under deep conviction." I went forward and gave my heart, my life, and my service to Jesus Christ. I was gloriously and unapologetically born again. The unfaltering prayers of Mom and Dad Ball were finally and fully answered. I became a new creation in Christ Jesus. It was the first stage of being rescued from that awful river and healed of its effects.

My new faith and my new last name made me "the *Day* the Lord has made" and I have rejoiced in it every since. Things didn't work out with the girl but the Lord and I have been together ever since. He gets more credit than me for that.

A couple of Sundays later, I told the pastor that I thought I was being "called to the ministry." He was an old-timey, hiccuping preacher who didn't have much education. His sermons were delivered so quickly and with such force that he sucked up air when he took a breath. The sound of that resembled a hiccup. He once preached so fast and so hard that he got a nosebleed but kept right on going until he was finished. He said to me, "Well, let's see. You can preach next Sunday night." I did. In every bit of ten minutes I told the faithful congregation everything I knew about the Bible, and speculated on a bunch of stuff I didn't. A young man made a decision for Christ that night. I took it as a sign that I was called to preach, and from that point on I planned on being an evangelist or a pastor. I had no idea what that really meant. Word spread about the "boy preacher" and I got several preaching engagements throughout the area, which was pretty heady for a young Christian.

Things were getting better in my heart but worse in my home. My newfound religion was not a big hit with my parents. I was like so many new converts; I was zealous to share my faith but sometimes too pushy about it. I tried witnessing to them. When that got no results, I left gospel tracts lying around the house. I even tried hiding them in the sandwich bags filled with dope. At that time Pete Day did not appreciate my concern for the lost souls looking to get high on some quality weed. He once told me to "Cool it with the Christianity bit or get out."

Following Jesus isn't easy. But it isn't complicated either. Either you do, or you don't.

My faith, my parents' troubled relationship, and our very different lifestyles constantly collided. But I made it to my graduation from Jellico High School, sane and intact. They dutifully attended. Then I got out of there as fast as I could.

It was spring 1980, the beginning of a new decade. The countercultural revolution that erupted in the 1960s would quickly give way to a resurgence of traditionalism. The "malaise" (as President Carter called it) of the 1970s would soon be replaced by a new optimism. 1980 represented a fresh start, and I was excited to begin living life on my own terms. My enthusiasm was bolstered by the realization that I would likely see 2001 and the birth of a new century. Despite my past, I would embark on my own odyssey into an unknown future, equipped with little more than my novice faith in Jesus. It was exhilarating.

With the help of the Shirleys, I went to work at a Christian camp for the summer. They were planning to leave the church and go back to their hometown and wanted someone to continue the mentorship they had started with me. At this time I had no plans to attend college. Earlier, I thought I had a football scholarship for a school in Tennessee, but my application was ultimately rejected based on my horrible grades and test scores. My overall ACT was a pitiful 14 of a possible 36. The math portion was only four. I would have done better just guessing the answers. Going to work at the camp was my escape. I had no clue what was coming next or how I was going to make it on my own.

Daymond and Joyce Helton managed what was then called Singing Hills Bible Camp. I fell in love with the camp and with them. The Heltons quickly filled the breach in my life and became like substitute parents to me. I learned a great deal from them. Daymond taught by example what Christian humility and service looked like. Mama Joyce, as I and many other people called her, taught me so many things, from how to pray in faith to how to purchase the right underwear brand. Both skills are useful for a good life. She also had to teach me to change my underwear every day and wash them once a week. A young man growing up the way I did doesn't know some of the basics.

I think we fail too many of the children who grow up in the

system at the critical time they are leaving it. When they turn eighteen they need parents just as much as they ever did before and in many ways even more. Transitioning to adulthood is where we lose a good number of them who, up to that time, might have had a fair chance to break the negative patterns and make a good life for themselves. However, before they have any opportunity, all the daily concerns of living come crashing down on them. They are sorely unprepared, under-resourced, and quickly discouraged. They go back to the only family they know for the only support they can find, and they get sucked into the old destructive influences and dysfunctional behaviors all over again.

The Heltons provided the tender guidance and tough love I needed most, just when I needed it most. We stayed close over the years. My children called them Grandma Joyce and Grandpa Daymond. They are the only grandparents on my side of the family that my children ever really knew. Mama Joyce died a few weeks after I became the Executive Director of Patrick Henry Family Services. Unlike when I heard the news about my mother's death just weeks earlier, I wept and mourned her loss. I still miss her. There are times I wish I could call and ask her for some advice and have her pray for me. I guess people never outgrow their need for a mom.

That first summer at Singing Hills began the second chapter of my life. It was there, on that God-blessed property that was once a home for abandoned children, that the building blocks of who I am and what I do today were laid.

#122. Calling

Ever wonder what it is you are supposed to do with your life? Do you know your "life's calling"? Answer two simple questions and you will have a very strong clue, if not a clear answer: 1. What do you cry about? 2. What do you laugh about?

In other words, what moves you? Think about the things that break your heart. Think about the things you are passionate about, so passionate that you are brought to tears when standing in the fullness of the need, or you laugh and shout for joy when seeing that need met.

You see, God has given each one of us a small slice of His heart, a tiny portion of the things He loves and cares about. He does that because He wants us to join Him in the work of meeting the needs of the world, to participate in the grand work of rescuing and restoring all things back to the created order. Doing anything else is falling short of our calling.

StraightTalkwithRobertDay.org

I met Vic Edwards at camp the week he served as pastor. He was a professor of religion at the college I used to walk through on my way to school. As the week unfolded, he learned more about me, my background, my current situation, and my desire to be in the ministry. After several conversations spanning the summer, he finally convinced me that I needed a college education. I told him I didn't have the money and I had only a few old clothes. I also explained that I didn't have the time or the knowledge to fill out the necessary paperwork. He pleaded with me that if I would just show up on a certain day, everything would be taken care of for me. I was willing to try. I had nowhere else to go and I was not going back home.

He lived up to the deal. I arrived on the specified day and found that I was registered as a student and had a dorm room. I had a set of new clothes hanging in the closet and an envelope on the bed with some cash in it. All of that, and I never completed one single form! He gave me a hug and said it was now all up to me. He continued to check on me and provide guidance. He was my professor, my mentor, and my friend during those years of enlightenment.

Vic knew I had some preaching experience, so he booked me to do a mini-revival at the church he was pastoring. I always appreciated how he found ways to develop leadership in me and in his other students. Unfortunately, I was quite the embarrassment. First, I made a bunch of flyers promoting the revival and then plastered them all over the community. There was nothing wrong with that, except I had misspelled the words Baptist and Revival and had one of the dates wrong. Second, I made a fool of myself on the very first night. As I got up to preach, I headed back to the vestibule to ring the church bell. It was to serve as an illustration, but the point was lost when I failed to let go of the rope on the second hard pull and it jerked me up in the air just as the congregation turned around to see what I was doing. All they could see were my dangling legs. Red-faced, I continued as if I meant to do it all along.

College was awesome! Although I was only twelve miles down the road from where I lived last, I might as well have been in another part of the world. As they would say in the mountains, "I took a shine to it." I thought college was a lot like camp, only the fun kept getting interrupted by classes. Remember, I was never a good student. That didn't change just because I was in college.

In the summer after my first year, I had a fateful discussion with my roommate David Emmert about poverty. We were both taking the same summer class. One of our assignments was to read Ron Sider's book, *Rich Christians in an Age of Hunger*. I didn't know much about anything I was learning; philosophy, sociology, psychology, and theology were way over my head. I had no educational underpinning on which to base any conceptual understanding. However, I did know a thing or two about poverty and poor people. It was on that I could hang my hat.

David was what I could have been if I had been adopted by the Balls. I was what he might have been if he hadn't been adopted. He grew up in the stable Christian home of a medical doctor who adopted him when he was born. He had a hard time believing that there was third-world type of poverty in the United States.

One weekend I took him on a driving tour of the area. I showed him some of the places I had lived. He saw a family living in an old abandoned school bus and another living in what had previously been a chicken coop. He also saw dozens of tar paper shacks dotting the countryside. He was confronted that day with the ugly truth of poverty in Appalachia, and he asked a simple question: "Why isn't anything being done about it?"

Something done about it? For the first time in my life, I was challenged with the notion that something should and could be done about it. Poverty was all I had ever known. It was deeply rooted into my being, and it created all kinds of false assumptions on which my worldview was built. I was starting to see that not everyone grew up the way I did. At one level I knew that already. When I was younger, I often wondered about how people in nice houses lived, but I never thought that was for me or that it could be my future. You see, people don't live in reality. They live in the story they tell themselves about reality. The key is to change the narrative.

As a child, and even up through high school, my best dream was to drive a coal truck I owned and to live in a doublewide trailer in a nice mobile home park that had paved roads and a nice yard to mow. That was the extent, the boundary if you will, of my very small world. I am not criticizing anyone for where they live or what they do for a living. I'm simply saying that the farthest my imagination could take me was restricted at the time by my own needs and experience.

Poor people often remain poor because everyone they know is poor. Everyone thinks as they do and they think like everyone around them. Every person, place, and event in their narrow experience confirms their biased perceptions of how the world works and how (and where) they are to live in it. A person's view of the world is small when life itself is limited. My friend David, the Heltons, my greater college experience, and even my awful time in California were serving to expand the borders of my own comprehension. Simply said, my concept of the world was getting bigger and with it, my aspirations.

Our conversations about poverty continued as we tried to answer the question: "Why isn't anything being done about it?" David and I figured that *we* could do something. Heck, we could build better homes than what we saw just six miles from the college, and with that conclusion, Mountain Outreach was born. I had just turned 19.

We sought counsel from anyone who would listen. Jim Wilson, the campus minister, and Ron Zorn, a professor in the religion department, were especially supportive. We met Sister Noel, a Catholic nun who had been working with the area poor for decades. She was more than willing to assist us, as we were willing to assist the poor. She started by introducing us to Lee Leforce.

Lee was a 76-year-old veteran with mobility issues who lived on his ancestor's plot of land in a house without water or electricity, although it had it at one time. He was also caring for his 45-year-old intellectually disabled son, Arthur. A tree had fallen on the front of the house blocking the main entrance. The nuns asked if we could take that on as a project.

We spread the word around campus and had about a dozen people show up early on an autumn Saturday morning to help. We spent the day cutting and clearing away the tree and the head-high brush and weeds that were all around the house. In doing so, we discovered broken and missing windows, gaping holes in walls, and an interior that resembled a garbage dump that even my grandmother would have avoided.

We hauled out over 80 large garbage bags of trash just from the kitchen alone, where mangy dogs came in and out as they pleased.

David and I were carrying out the nasty mattress that Arthur slept on when a rat appeared from inside, jumped onto my chest, and then onto the ground. Lee was standing there and saw what had happened and simply said, "I've got rat problems." David and I looked at each other funny, smiled and kept working.

It was clear even to our untrained eyes that this was no place for those two to live. Before we left, the group decided that we would build them a house. We didn't know how we were going to do it, but youthful exuberance doesn't need to know the "how" of a thing; it only needs to know the "why" of a thing. That is the reason faith sometimes looks a lot like foolishness. There is a principle we try to live by at Patrick Henry Family Services: commitment precedes resources. I learned it during my days in Mountain Outreach. The Bible teaches that the economy of God is predicated on that principle.

As you can imagine, it wasn't easy getting things started. We had no money other than what David could spend from his own allowance. Most of the first tools purchased for Mountain Out-reach came from him personally. We also used his truck to haul supplies, which were very difficult to obtain. We would beg, bor-row, or steal them. But the greatest challenge was finding people who had the time and the skills to help. The semester quickly came to an end and all we had constructed was the foundation and flooring for a simple two-room dwelling. Everyone went home for Christmas break with the commitment to continue when we returned. But over the break, the area was hit with an Arctic cold front that dropped temperatures down into the single digits for several days in a row.

On the first day back from break, I saw Pam Schumeth, one of our regular volunteers. We both expressed our concerns regard-ing Lee and Arthur, so we decided to skip our classes and head straight out and check on them. They lived only a few miles from the college, but actually getting to the house took quite an effort.

We had to park at the end of a dirt road, cross a small creek, and walk through a muddy field with waist-high brush, and then over a hill. The normal routine required that we stop and announce loudly to Lee that we were there, and he would come out and meet us. This time there was no response. After waiting a while, Pam and I went on to the house. We knocked and again, no response. We entered and found Arthur hidden and shivering under some filthy blankets and Lee lying on an old couch where he normally slept. He looked very sick.

I asked how he was doing. He told me the fire had gone out in the stove days before, and he couldn't get another one started. The firewood had actually frozen together, and a thin layer of ice covered the entire stack. Lee explained that his feet were hurting him "terribly bad." I requested that he let me take a look, but he was hesitant. Finally I insisted and started taking off his shoes. He reached down as I did and said, "I'm afraid they're going to fall off." I thought he meant his shoes but he meant his toes. He wasn't wearing socks, just a pair of well-worn shoes. His feet were black. His toes were a sickening white and red streaks were running up his legs. I had never seen it before, but I assumed it was frostbite.

I told Lee we had to get him to a hospital. He didn't want to go, but again I was insistent. I picked him up and carried him over the hill, through the field, across the creek, and into David's truck. Pam and I took him to the nearest hospital. As I drove, Pam started talking with him about the seriousness of his condition. She told him that she feared he would not only lose his feet but could also lose his life. She asked him if he was ready for death. He mumbled that he was not.

Lee and Pam had developed a true friendship during our weeks of work at his house. While others were clearing brush, digging footings, or laying floor, Pam visited with Lee and kept him company. She had earned the right to be heard. As we hurried down the road, Pam clearly and confidently shared with Lee the love of

Jesus Christ. She explained in very simple terms what was needed for him to be ready for eternity in heaven. I listened with amazement as the old mountain man from Kentucky prayed with the young college girl from Ohio for the salvation of his soul. They finished just as we drove up to the Emergency Room.

Just as Pam had predicted, Lee's feet were amputated that day in an effort to save his life. Sadly, his frailty and poor health were more than the doctors could overcome, and Lee died a couple of days later. The angels in heaven rejoiced, and I'm certain he did too, when Jesus showed him his new home.

The Mountain Outreach team was devastated. In our first effort to help, we had failed miserably. We were obviously on the right track—our intervention could have saved his life that winter. But we were too late—an American veteran died of frostbite he got while sleeping in his own home. We were deeply ashamed that our attempts to rescue him were unsuccessful.

But the Lord turned what we thought was a defeat into a wonderful victory.

A local newspaper somehow heard about what happened and ran a story about the small group of college students trying to make a difference for the poor in the area. That story got picked up by other news outlets. Soon other students responded to the news by asking how they could help. People we didn't know gave us donations of tools, materials, and cash. Churches started getting involved. Our motivations were renewed and we decided to give it another try.

The second time we decided to build a new home for a young couple and their toddler who lagged far behind in walking and other motor skills. They lived in a one-room structure that had once served as a tool shed. It had a bed and one chair. The head of the bed touched one wall and the foot of the bed touched the other. When you opened the only door, it would hit the side of the bed.

This time the house went up in relatively short order because of all the help. It cost less than $3,000 to construct, but it had two bedrooms, a living room, and kitchen. The baby had plenty of room to learn how to walk. It also had electricity, something they did not have in their previous "house." But it did not have running water. That was something beyond our funds and expertise but not really expected in that area at that time. We did, however, build a nice new outhouse that they appreciated nearly as much as the new house.

That summer, one year after our fateful discussion, we built five new homes with the help of church youth groups. Each group raised the funds to build part of the house they volunteered to work on. Groups have been coming every summer since 1982. Mountain Outreach carries on today after more than three decades. It's still led by 18-to-24-year-old college students. They have built hundreds of very nice homes (with running water), distributed tons of new clothes and toys, drilled many wells for fresh drinking water, and completed hundreds of weatherization projects, all in the desire to improve the lives of the poor, especially the children.

Pam and my roommate David married, and I had the great honor of performing the wedding ceremony, my first. Later they served as missionaries in Ethiopia for over a decade. They now serve a church in Florida.

Through my work at Mountain Outreach I met my beautiful wife Karen. After we both graduated from Cumberland College, we went to seminary, where I got a Master's in Social Work and later a Master's of Divinity. God has blessed us with four wonderful children and a good life of service to others. While it took a number of years for me to get completely free from my traumatic past, my children have never experienced any of the things I did growing up, and I consider that my single, greatest achievement.

All the horrible, awful, ugly things that happened to me as a child have ultimately worked out for the good. I can see that very clearly now. Not everything has necessarily resulted in my good, though, and that's okay. I hope I'm not doing the scripture an injustice, but the promise is that "in all things God works for the good of those who love him, who have been called according to his purposes." I went through some bad things as a child, and that has resulted in others experiencing the good that I have learned from them. My passion to serve vulnerable children and distressed families is the greatest good that has come from my suffering. The Lord has given a purpose to the pain of my past. God has been good to me. Always.

I also am convinced that when the Kingdom of God comes in all of its fullness and glory, everything that has been lost to sin and stolen by Satan will be returned and restored to those who love him and are called according to his purpose.

I fear that few, if any, of my family will be in heaven. My blood relatives will miss out on The Restoration of all things, because they did not accept the blood sacrifice of Jesus Christ as a gracious gift for their sin.

Nonetheless, I will have family there. George and JoAnne Ball will be my parents. Daymond and Joyce Helton will be my grandparents. Doris Brown will be my aunt, Vic Edwards my uncle. The Shirleys will be my cousins, and the Emmerts my siblings. I will live in a community of extended family members made up of dozens of people, many I no longer remember, but I will know them then. I will live peacefully in a community filled with loving individuals who touched my life in many kind and thoughtful ways, precious folks I never had a chance to thank. The Lord has chosen my inheritance (Ps. 47:4).

Sin devastated my family of origin. Satan destroyed my culture and ravished my community. But God, through his church, filled in the gaps for me here on earth. In heaven, he will fully restore it all.

One fine day I will live in a place of unimaginable prosperity, where there are no social workers or police. They won't be needed. There will be no need for therapists or drug counselors, doctors or child abuse investigators either. The place I am going will be enjoyed for what is not there as much as for what is.

Until then, however, I will continue to work hard to bring the Kingdom of Heaven here on earth, to return what was lost in the Garden of Eden. To not strive for that here and now would make me unworthy of living there and then. Please don't misunderstand. I know without a doubt that I am saved by grace and do not need to earn God's love or the right to possess the joys of heaven. That has been settled once and for all on the cross. It's just that I am so exceedingly grateful for that amazing grace that I want to bring a little bit of that glorious kingdom to as many children and families as I can. For me, at least, anything other than working for the good, rescuing as many as possible from that social problem river, is an appalling waste of time and energy.

What are you going to do?

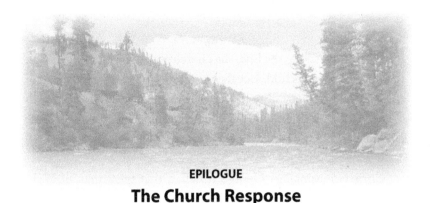

EPILOGUE

The Church Response

To neglect that mission is to negate the message.

M Y STORY IS NOT UNIQUE. It wasn't unique when I was a kid. It's still not unique today, and that's precisely the problem. What happened to me, and far worse, is happening to an ever-increasing number of children. The outcomes for these little ones are more in question than ever before. I was fortunate in many ways. I was blessed with several local churches and many good Christian people in my life who took an interest in me and helped me along the way. It was not coordinated in any conceivable method, but it nevertheless was part of God's orchestrated plan.

I fear, though, that the church is shrinking in size and influence, and that means fewer opportunities for children with challenges like mine to get the assistance they need from the community best-equipped to help them. I also believe there is a direct link between the dying church and the loss of its special purpose.

The church must be clearer with its message. I'm firmly convinced of that. There is no substitute for unapologetically preaching the Word, confidently proclaiming the Gospel, and zealously participating in evangelistic efforts. None! At the same time, I am equally convinced that the church has a biblically mandated social responsibility as well, one that has as its core purpose meeting the needs of children (and, by extension, the needs of families). To neglect that mission is to negate the message.

Somewhere along the line, the church abandoned its special call to love the unloved child. Local congregations have largely rejected their distinct responsibility to serve the abandoned child, the social orphan, the unwanted kid. In doing so, their religion has become defiled and their power in the world sorely diminished.

It wasn't always this way.

Christian evangelist George Mueller, that great man of faith who served as director of Ashley Down Orphanage in Bristol, England, a century ago, was responsible for caring for over ten thousand orphans in his day. He also established 117 schools that offered Christian education to over 120,000 children, many of them orphans. That is a truly amazing accomplishment by any standard.

Mueller had two firm convictions that provided purpose for his life and motivation for his work. First, he believed that by faith all things are possible. He never let anyone know his needs but God, and then he waited to see how the Lord would provide. In other words, he believed in the principle "commitment precedes resources." His remarkable achievements are a clear testimony to his faith and to that powerful proposition.

Second, he fervently believed that caring for and serving children in need was the very best investment anyone could make for the world and for the Kingdom of God. He famously said, "The power for good or evil that resides in a little child is great beyond all human calculation. A child rightly trained may be a world-wide blessing. But a neglected or misdirected child may live to blight and blast mankind."

Mueller was absolutely right. The future of our nation, or of any nation for that matter, is determined by how children are treated—pure and simple. If we neglect, abuse, or exploit them, we will inherit a society reflective of that treatment. If we sow the wind in the lives of children, the prophet Hosea suggests we will reap a whirlwind in our own lives as well as the lives of those who come after us. Jesus said that it would be better to hang a millstone around our necks than to cause one of his children to stumble.

A modern champion for children, Marian Wright Edelman, a child of poor Mississippi sharecroppers and founder of The Children's Defense Fund, states the proposition squarely: "The future which we hold in trust for our own children will be shaped by our fairness to other people's children."

Methodist minister Charles Loring Brace, who is considered the father of the modern foster care movement, understood better than most what George Mueller meant. Brace founded The Children's Aid Society but is most renowned for starting the Orphan Train Movement, which lasted from 1854 to 1929. It all began when he personally witnessed thousands of derelict children in New York City who lived in dire poverty, with parents who engaged in criminal activity and were in many ways unfit. These children were sent to beg for money on the streets in order to survive. They became known as "the dangerous classes" due to the street violence and gangs of which they inevitably became a part. In some cases, children as young as five years old would be sent to jails where adults were imprisoned. The police referred to these children as "street rats" and treated them very badly.

Brace had a vision and solution. He said, "The best of all asylums for the outcast child is the farmer's home. The great duty is to get these children of unhappy fortune utterly out of their surroundings and to send them away to kind Christian homes in the country."

We are shocked today to think of how those Orphan Trains operated. Yet ponder the bleak alternative. Our modern sensitivities are easily offended by the picture of countless orphans lined up at the railway stations, shortest to the tallest, being inspected like cattle by prospective parents. However, it is far better than leaving them to die on the streets or live a lifetime of crime and poverty.

I admire Reverend Brace. He was enough of an idealist that he could envision a better future for those children, yet he was a pragmatist at the same time. He didn't let the perfect stand in the way of the good. Those defenseless children were in desperate need, and Brace found the most efficient and most cost-effective way to rescue as many as he could. He provided them with what they needed most. Over 200,000 children rode those trains to new families and new lives. The benefit to the nation is both immeasurable and indescribable.

I know it seems simplistic, and in a way it is, but it's that kind of common-sense approach that we are missing today. There is no money to be made in this type of straightforward solution, and so those in the child-welfare-industrial-complex will simply not be able to see beyond their self-preserving regulations.

But who cares? That should not stop us. Did God give the state the responsibility to care for needy children? No. He gave that magnificent privilege to us, His church. Yet we have become deaf to our call; we have denied our grand purpose. The power-hungry politicians and their unimaginative bureaucrats who carry out their trophy laws now do what only we are meant to do. The social activists and the social workers, like so many others in the helping professions, have commodified these vulnerable children in order either to make a buck, to make a point, or to make "progressive" changes in society. Meanwhile, we in the Body of Christ have largely forsaken the powerless ones and, by doing so, have doomed the church to irrelevance and doomed our culture to the curse of unruly and expendable children. Shame on us!

Imagine though, for a moment, all the children rescued by Mueller in England and Brace in the United States. Not only did these two remarkable servants of God, with the help of a vast network of God's people, rescue hundreds of thousands of children in their day, but they also blessed their respective countries for generations to come. They saved their nations untold harm. Those children grew up to be blessings instead of curses, and more likely than not, to raise decent children of their own. The significance of their work echoes down through the generations in ways only God himself knows.

I cannot think of a more honorable service, with the greatest impact, for the most people, than to help a helpless child. C.S. Lewis believed that "Children are not a distraction from more important work. They are the most important work."

Perhaps there is no one with more evangelistic credentials than Charles Haddon Spurgeon. The "Prince of Preachers" is world-renowned in Christendom for his solid, soul-winning preaching. Yet Spurgeon loved the work of caring for the fatherless and believed it was a crucial service of the local church. Once, after delivering a sermon with the purpose of stirring up support for the orphanage he started, someone challenged his priorities. Spurgeon's response is priceless. "Sir, usually I do preach for souls, but my orphans cannot eat souls. And if they could, it would take four souls the size of yours to make a square meal for just one orphan!" The orphanage he began 150 years ago is now the UK's leading children's charity, serving around 37,000 annually.

For decades the best known children's home in the United States was Boys Town, just outside of Omaha, Nebraska. The 1938 film *Boys Town,* starring Spencer Tracy, made it famous. But it was their method and especially their success at changing the life and direction of these boys that gave it the well-deserved reputation of being the model for working with troubled youth.

In 1917, Irish-born Catholic priest Father Flannigan started Boys Town after years of working with vagrant men. He determined that it was "better to build a boy than to mend a man." His home for boys was truly distinctive in its day. Under his direction Boys Town grew to be a large community with its own boy-mayor, schools, and even with an official U.S. post office.

Flannigan revealed his effective philosophy when he said, "There are few rules which apply to all boys and their troubles. The individuality which I seek to develop in each boy calls for special consideration, the finding of the one particular remedy." I like that. Each child has his or her own particular remedy. It's a principle nearly extinct in our heavily regulated, institutional approaches today.

Evangelicals, mainline denominations, Protestant or Catholic—God's church all around the world—have been in the business of reaching, rescuing, and restoring children ever since Jesus rebuked his disciples for keeping the children from him.

Only two times in the gospels do we see Jesus angry. The most well-known of the two events is when he throws the money changers out of the Temple. Jesus was deeply incensed that his Father's house had been turned into a "den of thieves." The zeal Jesus showed that day for the purity of all things God was clearly evident.

The second time is when his own disciples turned away the parents who were bringing their children to be blessed by him. Mark's unique account of that story said that Jesus became indignant and rebuked them. Indignation is a special kind of anger. It is a belief or recognition of unfair treatment. The disciples were treating the children unfairly by not allowing them to come to Jesus, and that made him mad. How could these men, who spent so much time with him, not know his heart on that issue?

The two incidents have something in common. Both are symbols of the Kingdom of Heaven. The Temple was made of earthly materials, by human hands, but was designed to represent heaven, where God resided. The same could be said of children. As for their being a symbol of God's Kingdom, consider what Jesus said to his disciples: "Let the little children come to me, and do not hinder them, for such is the Kingdom of Heaven." He went on to claim that no one will enter heaven without being like a little child. Is he just speaking hyperbole? I don't think so.

Jesus of Nazareth wasn't just a nice guy who liked children and so we should too. Jesus was the Word of God Incarnate. He held children in the highest regard because of what they represent on earth. How the church treats children is what the church thinks about the Kingdom they serve.

Take an American flag, spit on it, then set it on fire. What will happen? It's only a piece of cloth. It doesn't cost a lot of money. Yet I think you understand the point I'm making. The power of the flag is its symbolism of something much greater. It represents an idea, a belief, a doctrine, a hope for a certain way of life. The people who believe and put their aspirations in those things will be gravely offended at your disrespectful treatment of their flag.

How people treat the flag says something about what they think of the country it represents. I believe the same is true of children. How we treat the most helpless among us speaks volumes about what we think of the Kingdom God has built for them, of their innocence, and of the loving father's heart for all.

The Lord's intimate concern for the fatherless goes all the way back to the time of Moses and the Law and is expressed throughout scripture. One of my favorite verses in the Bible is Psalm 27:10: "When my father and my mother forsake me, then the LORD will take me up."

In western civilizations based on a Judeo-Christian ethic, children fare the best—far better than their counterparts in other parts of the world. Why? These cultures discovered the concept of childhood in that sacred story of Jesus blessing the little ones.

The idea of childhood is not universal. Despite what others might claim, childhood was not invented by a capitalist society that could afford to carve out a special, privileged period of time for their offspring. Childhood was discovered in sacred text. Throughout human history, and even today in many parts of the world, children are treated as small adults. They are forced to work, consume, war, and have sex like adults. In our own country, we see these destructive attitudes rising as the church's influence diminishes. I firmly believe that the fate of children is connected to the strength of the church. The strength of the church is bound to its conduct toward children.

Bolstered then by such a great cloud of witnesses, and by such a clarion call to bless the children, what are we going to do?

You may ask, "What can a local church do with such a complex problem? What can one individual Christian do to make any real difference?" The answer—a great deal more than you might think. It doesn't need to be complex like operating Orphan Trains, or costly like running an orphanage. It just needs to be what God is calling you to do—nothing more and nothing less. Since he is already doing the work, he will provide what you need. You are simply joining him in his work.

I'm not going to list here all the possible ways you or your church can help the needy children in your area. That's for you and your church, civic group, or ministry to figure out. Put on your thinking cap. Brainstorm with others. Pray. Seek God's guidance. It may be something already being done or something entirely new. That's the beauty of it. It can be a targeted approach or something with broad appeal. It can be something that requires specialization or something anybody can do. It's really up to you. What is the Lord putting on your heart? The point is to roll up your sleeves and dive into the river. There is plenty to do. Just get busy.

Every church, civic group, or ministry, no matter its size or resources, is enriched when it fulfils God's mission. But more practically, when churches and believers step out in faith to care for those in need, they grow spiritually and God blesses their obedience. They move out of the "ME box" and become more mindful of others, living sacrificially and laying down their lives. All this makes a church more meaningful to a community. It also brings a sense of unity and cooperation as members work together to meet the needs of children and families. I have always believed that a healthy self-interest is better than a flabby altruism.

Outlined below are seven principles to help you filter your ideas. Meet these foundational criteria and you can be assured your ministry to needy children will be on the right track.

#81. Main Thing

You have probably heard it said that "the main thing is to keep the main thing the main thing." I agree. That's absolutely, positively right. But the essential question remains. What is the main thing?

I firmly believe that the main thing is the mission, your mission. In other words, "the main thing is to keep your mission the main thing." But that leads to a second, equally important, question. What is your mission? What is your main thing? Only you can answer that question. No one else can do it for you.

Each and every human being was created for a purpose, gifted for a reason, and called to a unique purpose. Knowing, understanding, submitting to and working towards that mission, that task, that special assignment, is the main thing. It is a mission that is as common as snowfall and as unique as a snowflake, and when you learn to keep it the main thing you will live an extremely rare but wonderfully blessed life.

StraightTalkwithRobertDay.org

Being a good Baptist preacher, I have found a way to make a complete seven-point argument and make each point start with the same letter. I apologize if that seems weird to you, but it's an old habit. Use whatever words make most sense to you. Also, feel free to add anything to the list you find missing.

1. **Compassion**: Make sure that your work with children is based on a foundation of compassion and grace. Rules are necessary and structure is essential when working with kids. They may act like they don't want structure, but they do and they certainly need it. However, ministry to children must not be rules-based but grace-based and filled with true compassion for them. It should be led by those who actually like them. There is something about children and dogs—they instinctively know if someone cares for them and if someone does not. Be compassionate and let it show.

Speak it to them. Live it in front of them. Be careful, though, not to let your compassion overrule wisdom and prudence, especially in these days of hypersensitivity. But if you are going to err, I believe in erring on the side of love.

2. **Child-focused**: It kind of makes sense that a ministry to children should be focused on the children, but that's not always the case. Children are often pawns in someone else's game. To some they are a means to achieve an end. If your ministry to children is constantly adjusting to the needs and desires of the adults in charge, then it is adult-focused and not child-focused. You should filter all of your ministry decisions through this question: Is this in the best interest of children? If you can truly answer in the affirmative, then move forward. If not, then rethink what you're doing. Yes, you may end up having to replace the carpet. It's true that something is going to get torn up. Things are going to break. Yet what is that in comparison to the life of even one child? What is that in the light of eternity?

3. **Closeness**: All ministry requires closeness. It must touch people where they live and be meaningful to their lives. It must be community-based, culturally sensitive, and developmentally appropriate. We can't sit in our pews, doing church our way, and expect children just to show up. Sometimes they might, but they won't keep coming back if their experience there isn't close to the reality they know. As much as possible, ministry to children must go to where children live, be relevant to how they live, and meet the immediate and long-term needs in their precious lives. The ultimate goal is to challenge how they live, to have them take a critical look at their culture and life, but first you have to meet them where they are. Bottom line: ministry to children cannot be done at a distance. It involves getting down on your knees, in their dirty little faces, and in their sometimes strange developing minds.

4. **Connection**: Allied to the concept of closeness is the need for connection. This is an especially critical component when

working with older children and teenagers. Adults working with youth must find ways to relate to them. Caution—don't try too hard. Relating to kids does not mean acting like kids. They don't need you to be their friend, and they certainly don't want you acting childish, but they do need you to be a caring adult. They would rather you be genuine than cool. It's been my experience that young people hate hypocrisy and they can smell it a mile away. So just be you, but in all your "you-ness" find ways to connect with them and their world. It requires a great amount of energy and creativity, but it's possible.

5. **Commitment**: Don't start working with vulnerable children unless you're committed. All children need consistency, but especially children who are at-risk. They need adults who keep promises. Ministry to children must be led by caring adults who will stay for the "long haul." It's not so much a matter of time as it is a matter of circumstances, especially for children with behavior problems. Many adults get scared and quit. Others are frightened away by their own high moral standards. For some people, their very Christianity gets in the way of doing the hard, messy work of helping troubled children and their dysfunctional families. The commitment required is nothing less than unconditional love and unquestioned acceptance. If you think you might have a difficult time with that, then do the children a favor and serve somewhere else.

6. **Control**: It's the opposite of chaos, and children need it more than ever. Remember, we aren't talking so much about *rules* as we are about *order*. Children must feel safe and must actually be safe—physically, emotionally, and spiritually. There must be predictability in our ministry to children. It's really about providing a secure and stable environment. Be sure the adults are safe and are not threatening in any way. If someone is unwilling to submit to a background check or ongoing supervision, then he or she has no business serving children. People with good intentions have no problem with accountability.

7. **Christian:** This should go without saying. The single greatest need of any child is Jesus. There are many good and positive things that groups and individuals can do for children that don't necessarily have anything to do with Christianity. Recreation, for example, has value in and of itself. Yet the one thing a church or Christian group can give to children, the one thing they cannot get anywhere else, is knowledge of the Savior. He is the ultimate rescuer of their lives. Introducing children to Jesus is the best gift we can give them. However, if we simply do that and do not attempt to meet their other needs, we most likely will fail at both.

So let's wrap this up as concisely as possible.

First the bad news. Despite our spending billions of dollars on childcare, education, the fight on poverty, and everything else under the sun, America's children still face a bleak future. Every pathological tendency in the culture is being visited on our children at earlier and earlier ages. The traditional family is at risk of becoming extinct as "alternative" families gain ascendancy, touting other kinds of relationships and lifestyles that are proving to be devastating to children. A teen suicide rate that has quadrupled in recent decades is ample evidence. Unless we find a way to make childhood possible again, unless we make a way to restore the traditional family, unless we find the collective will to stand against the rising tide of destruction that is persistent in our society, the future for our children is very bleak. We must act now!

High dropout rates, young women in poverty as heads of households, violent crimes and rampant drug use by undisciplined youths—all mutually reinforcing and self-perpetuating pathologies—have become our most pressing social problems. The change that took place in our culture during the last five decades is now accelerating. The temptations and problems that are destroying our youth are coming at them at quicker speeds. We live in exponential times, therefore we must speed up our efforts.

Now the good news. We will end with it. That is the way of the gospel.

Children are remarkably resilient. They have a lot of built-in survival skills. Fortunately, because of that special God-made elasticity, it takes very little to change a child's life for the better. Many successful adults who had difficult childhoods can remember a pivotal experience, or a special person, that allowed them to turn their troubled lives around. For some it was an adult who showed confidence in them. For others it might have been a summer camp that expanded their self-image.

For some it was the friendly neighborhood Kool-Aid mom who fed them when they were hungry. For some it may have been a safe place, like a local church, that nurtured their spirit and allowed them to express their ideas and talents. And for others still, it was a teacher who didn't give up on them. You know, it really doesn't take much to turn a life around. It doesn't always take a lot of resources—but it does always take caring and a willingness of adults to intervene.

The Bible informs us that God does not use human standards when calling his people to service: not many of us are considered wise, not many are considered powerful, not many come from royalty, to paraphrase from 1 Corinthians.

Are you an intellectual? Are you rich or powerful? Are you famous? Probably not, and that's okay. Being none of those things puts you in a great place, because God likes to use folks like you. God does have his celebrities. He does have some of the rich and famous who serve him. But for every one of them, there are thousands of ordinary people like you who are doing extraordinary things in this world. Just regular folks like you and me, quietly meeting needs, serving others, providing hope, and making a real difference in the world.

Together we can do this. We must do this, for the children's sake and for our own.

What are you going to do?

Common Sense or Death:
The Patrick Henry Way

WHETHER IT'S IN THE ARENA OF POLITICS, economics, education, or jurisprudence, our culture seems to be losing all ability to make common-sense decisions. Oftentimes, when I watch or read the news, I feel like screaming. It seems that we are losing our collective minds.

There's no place where this is more evident to me than in the area of child welfare. Here are but a few examples:

A child is banned for life from a doughnut shop because he asked a woman in line if she was pregnant. She wasn't. He was four.

A mother was issued a misdemeanor for leaving her daughter in the car while she went into a store. The alert, responsive, eleven-year-old girl had asked to stay in the car.

Child Protective Services threatened to take an elementary-age child away because the parents refused to take him for a psychological exam after he got into trouble at school for "spinning a pencil like a gun."

A preschool forced a three-year-old deaf child to change his name because his sign-language gesture looks like a weapon.

One mom was arrested for letting her nine-year-old play in a park unsupervised. There was legitimate cause for concern since the child played while her mother worked her shift at a nearby McDonald's. However, instead of helping this poor, single mother with child care, they put her in jail and the child in foster care. McDonald's fired her. How is this helping anybody?

A judge gave probation for a teen who killed four people while driving drunk. The court determined he should not serve jail time because he was too rich and spoiled to know right from wrong. Later his mother helped him escape to Mexico to avoid the confines of his probation.

When it comes to the welfare of children we seem to have lost all common sense in this country. Political correctness, zero-tolerance, mind-numbing regulations, and a hypertensive fear of the state are robbing children of their childhood and parents of the confidence required to raise them in natural and nurturing ways.

For children to be healthy there are certain needs that must be met. They need appropriate physical contact, but everyone is now terrified to hug or touch them. They need loving discipline, but everyone's too scared to set limits, to say no and mean it. They need to learn morality, but everyone is now afraid of offending those who aren't moral, or they falsely believe other people's morals are not any of their business. This is crazy!

Here is a truth that many might find inconvenient. Morality is a public issue, not merely a private matter. Here are some examples.

Adultery, something that most people would classify as a private matter, requires more trials that are supported by taxes. More taxes for more trials makes adultery a public issue.

One household becoming two because of divorce not only means more trials but often means more poverty as well—since the wife often falls into poverty. We all pay a price for poverty, and no one doubts that poverty is a public issue. Divorce, because of its connection with courts and poverty, becomes a public issue.

Teen pregnancy generally means more welfare and therefore that makes sexual promiscuity a public issue.

Get my point? Most so-called private moral choices have very real public consequences. We all pay a price one way or another for moral decisions. In any community, every member matters and it matters what every member does. It really is our business.

But it's not just a failure to teach our children morality. It gets even worse.

We have labeled, medicated, and turned our most vulnerable children into commodities, especially the poor and needy. It's not just the big corporations making profits selling harmful junk to kids, or pop-culture turning them into small sexualized adults, but it's also those who are charged with their care and protection that are guilty. The more labels they can put on children, the more money it releases into the system for services. There is good money to be made serving bad kids, and there are many going after it.

There is ready cash to be made in all the social problems these days, and "helping" troubled and needy children is one of the most lucrative. Endless government subsidies have had the unintended consequence of creating a massive and powerful thirteen-billion-dollar child-welfare-industrial-complex. And, just like the stock market, those making money from the varied problems of children have to keep a close eye on the pendulum of politics to see where the money is flowing. Many who serve needy children are really chasing after the money instead of their mission, and they're twisting their programs in all sorts of odd ways in order to fit the criteria of the next government subsidy.

The love of money truly is the root of all sorts of evil against children.

Raising and caring for children isn't easy. But it isn't hard either. By that I mean that serving the needs of children is not that complicated. Yet somehow we have been sold a bill of goods in this country. We have been convinced that meeting the needs of children is so complex and complicated that it should be left up to the experts and professionals, to the government authorities and progressive educators who see children as not much more than a means to an end.

Enough already!

Something has to happen to turn this around, for all of our sakes. But our hope will not be found in some kind of big, dramatic solution, and we cannot wait for someone else to fix it. There is no grand plan, no noble leader who can save us from ourselves. There are not enough experts, or enough money, to throw at the problem.

Cultures change, for better or worse, because of of the countless small choices of millions of people. Every citizen matters, and it matters what every citizen decides. We will only restore this culture one decision at a time. It has to be done retail, not wholesale — person by person, family by family, community by community. More tax money for more government programs is not the answer. Congress cannot pass a law, no matter how comprehensive, that will repair it. While leadership is important, it will not matter what party is in power or who is occupying the Oval Office.

It's going to take a massive infusion of common sense and Christian principles into the cultural bloodstream. It's like fighting cancer. The cure will only come by restoring cell by cell until the entire body is healthy once again.

It's time we rise up together and demand (to use a concept from Patrick Henry) common sense or death. Without common sense there is only more insanity to come, and if we don't return to a more reasonable and rational approach to child welfare we are going to be so broke in this nation, and our children so troubled, that there will be no sustainable future for any of us. At that point we might as well sign our own death certificate.

Climate change? I'm more alarmed by the change in our culture and the condition of our children than by rising temperatures or sea levels. Children are the future. They will set the climate of our culture and the temperature of our well-being — for good or evil. Everything else, in my opinion, is just a side-effect.

At Patrick Henry Family Services, we are purposely different. We serve the needs of children in more reasonable and natural ways. Our program is quite simple really.

1. We provide a safe and nurturing, family-like, environment.
2. We teach and promote strong character.
3. We emphasize the importance of work.
4. We stimulate a carefree childhood.
5. We focus on academic success.
6. We provide religious instruction.
7. We love.

We provide quality care for susceptible children with a variety of challenges. We offer counseling when needed, provide appropriate discipline when necessary, and always show unconditional love and support.

To us they are not commodities. We don't take children into our program because there is money that comes with them. In fact, it's just the opposite. We have to find private funds to care for them. We don't view them as a diagnosis or a label, and we don't put them into psychological categories or treat them like patients (or victims). They are children—uniquely created individuals with gifts and strengths, needs and wants, and each of them has a special purpose to fulfill in the world.

We do all of this at a fraction of the expense of those programs taking government funding, while never turning any child, or family, away for financial reasons. It's truly a unique and remarkable ministry.

We here at Patrick Henry Family services are committed to the long haul. We are doing the difficult task of rescuing children and restoring families—one by one, day after day, until the job is done. And we do it without government funding.

Our vision is to meet the needs of every child before us, resulting in the maximum impact for the child, in the shortest time possible, in the most efficient way possible, always in a loving and professional manner.

These Things We Believe

I**T'S OUR FIRM BELIEF** at Patrick Henry Family Services that each child is a unique individual, created, gifted, and loved unconditionally by God, with his or her own special interests, talents, and purpose in life. Therefore we value and respect the dignity and integrity of each child who arrives on our campuses, camps, and counseling centers.

We understand and accept that all children have inherent and learned weaknesses, that they have been tainted by sin and, to some extent, are products of their "fallen" environment. However, we purposely choose to focus on a child's strengths instead of weaknesses, the positives instead of the negatives, and the good instead of the bad.

We also believe that children and their families are active, not passive, participants in their own helping process. We emphasize strengths as a way to foster motivation for growth. We assess their God-given assets to develop informed, achievable objectives for every plan of care. Children and families who come to any of our ministries for help must be enabled to make their own changes. We can't make people change. Nevertheless, we can help them decide to change by helping them value themselves, set achievable goals, and create a plan to reach those goals, creating a real potential to be successful. We also believe that process is immeasurably more likely to occur when aided by spiritual means and practices.

"Change your thinking, change your life" summarizes the approach we take at Patrick Henry Family Services. We believe behaviors flow from attitudes and attitudes are the natural by-products of a person's thought-life. If we can effectively change the way an individual unproductively thinks about himself, others, and how the world works, we can constructively modify the way that person treats himself, acts toward others, and ultimately succeeds in the world.

At Patrick Henry Family Services we believe that resources are everywhere. That means we accept as true that there is no person, environment, or situation where there are absolutely no resources. With that firmly held conviction, we do not concentrate on what is missing or what is needed in the person or environment, but rather on what positive resources are available.

This Strength-Based Philosophy motivates our ministry and guides every aspect of our programming. It, of course, stands in stark contrast to the medically oriented disease and pathology models that so permeate today's juvenile treatment centers. We believe our strategy is not only more optimistic in its outlook, but is also aligned with biblical teaching and basic common sense.

At Patrick Henry Family Services we believe that every child has the right to be viewed as a person capable of changing, growing, and becoming positively connected to a community, no matter what types of behaviors or challenges he or she has. We believe each one has a right to participate in the selection of services that will build on inherent gifts and mitigate flaws.

We believe that children have a right to contribute things they are good at and other strengths in all assessment and treatment processes. They also have a right, we believe, to have their resistance viewed as a message that the wrong approach may be being used with them. Instead of asking, "What's wrong with this child?" we ask, "What happened to this child?" That does not, however, absolve children of the responsibility for their poor behavior. We believe real transformation begins with accountability. But this shift of focus from the *individual* to the *individual's behavior* helps us to see "a child with a problem" rather than "a problem child."

We also believe that focusing on a person's past has some merit, but it's ultimately not the solution. Our interventions are more future-oriented. We believe in a helping process that concentrates on the real possibilities that lie ahead, rather than on what did or did not happen before. It is our well-founded conviction, yea our mission, to give children and families a future bursting with hope. We do that by giving them essential resources to be successful. If we manage to accomplish this, then their history no longer has consequence.

At Patrick Henry Family Services we believe children have the right to learn from their mistakes and to have support to learn that mistakes don't really mean failure. We believe that before people can forgive others, something every person must learn in order to be emotionally healthy, they must first learn to forgive themselves. We also believe that we should view their maladaptive or antisocial behaviors as a lack of skills, or faulty coping mechanisms, and that they can acquire the skills and adaptive tools needed to alter their lives for the better.

We believe that children have the right to experience success and to have support in connecting their previous successes to positive future goals. We also believe they have the right to have their culture and gender included as a strength and obtain services that honor and respect their culture and gender.

At Patrick Henry Family Services we believe that children have a right to be helped by professionals who view youth positively (by adults who actually like them), and to be served by caring individuals who understand that motivating children and youth is related to successfully tapping into their inner strengths. We believe that connection precedes correction and that those serving young people must first "earn the right to be heard." We also believe that they have the right not to be talked down to or to be talked about in a disparaging manner. They have a right to confidentiality and to have all needed communication about them to be constructive.

Children have a right, we believe, to have their family always involved in their experience in a way that acknowledges and supports their strengths as well as their deficits, and they have a right to stay connected to their family no matter what types of challenges they face. It's our conviction that the best family for all children is their own family, the best home is their own home. Therefore, we make it our top priority to return children to their home and restore them to their family if at all possible and as soon as possible.

At Patrick Henry Family Services we believe that all children everywhere have the right to be viewed and treated as a redeemable resource, a potential leader, and a success of the future. We furthermore believe that children have a right to be regarded and treated as more than a commodity, a statistic, a stereotype, a risk score, a diagnosis, a label, or a pathology. We believe they have a right to a future free of involvement by institutions or systems and to evidence-based services that most centrally and progressively focus on their successful transition from institutions.

We believe at Patrick Henry Family Services that children have the right to service providers who professionally coordinate their efforts and who share a united philosophy and treatment goal. We also believe that children have the right to exercise their developmental tasks at every stage without ridicule or shame, to try out new identities, and to practice their gifts in an encouraging atmosphere, free from the fear of rejection.

We enthusiastically embrace the commonly held belief among cultures grounded on a Christian worldview that childhood is a special, privileged period and therefore should be preserved and protected at all cost. We believe that every child has a right to a carefree childhood, absent from the burden of adult concerns, ideas, and activities. This means children should be allowed and stimulated to play, explore, imagine, laugh, sing, and, when appropriate, be silly. Children should never be punished for doing childish things. We also believe, though, that children must learn to be accountable, to say "I'm sorry" for the harm they've caused others, and to make amends for their hurtful behavior whenever possible.

We steadfastly believe that all children have promise, that they are fully capable of becoming kind, thoughtful, and productive citizens. But we also believe that does not happen without purposeful guidance, consistent discipline, and lots of moral instruction. Children should be taught to respect others, to work and contribute, to be responsible, and to be people of good character and strong principles.

Lastly, and most importantly, we strongly believe that children have both the basic human need and the God-given right to know without a doubt that they are loved, that they are wanted, that they are somebody and belong to somebody. Children thrive and prosper, we believe, only when they are secure in that knowledge and feel completely safe to be themselves, warts and all.

Family Pictures

As you can imagine, someone with my upbringing will not have many childhood photos, but I offer what I have to help bring the story alive.

*Robby sitting on the picnic table in front of
Mom and Dad Ball's home with the family dog.*

Mom Ball holding Robby in her lap at their Tennessee farm.

Robby with Dad Ball right after his first haircut.

Bobby (as he was called by the Brown family) and Aunt Moe
in the doorway of their Sioux City, Iowa home.

Everett Brown (Cora Wood's first husband)
outside his Sioux City, Iowa home.

After getting in trouble with Social Services, Cora Brown returned Robby to the Balls for a short stay. Robby and his mother are photographed on Easter Sunday with Mom and Dad Ball.

*Mom and Dad Ball come to visit a not very happy Robby who was
again living with his mother, this time in a trailer park.*

Cora with her third husband, Charles "Pete" Day,
Robert's adoptive father.

*Robert at his high school graduation with the friends
who helped him conduct the money-making scheme
to raise funds for him to travel back to Iowa.*

Robert with his half-brother, Joe Brown, on the day of their mother's funeral near the place where they both had suffered childhood abuse. Joe committed suicide about a year later.

Robert, center, with his four half brothers:
Leslie, Randy, David, and Joe Brown.

Robert with a group of assembled Mountain Outreach volunteers
one Saturday morning before heading out to the day's project.
His wife Karen is in the background, as is his long-time friend Drew.

*Robert's first Mountain Outreach project was to provide Lee,
a 76-year-old veteran with mobility issues, better housing
than his home photographed above.*

Lee watches as his new home is assembled
by the Mountain Outreach volunteers.

Daymond and Joyce Helton

Robert Day with his wife, Karen, and their four children,
Faith, Naomi, Sharon, and Alec.

About the Author

ROBERT J. DAY
MSW, MDV

Married
Father of 4
CEO of Patrick Henry Family Services
Host of Straight Talk Radio
Author

BORN TO AN UNWED, TEENAGED MOTHER, Robert's childhood of poverty and abuse included more than 35 temporary homes before his unlikely graduation from high school. Today, through God's grace, and with two Masters degrees in hand, Robert's life work is dedicated to keeping children safe and families strong. As CEO of Patrick Henry Family Services, Robert is successfully leading the organization to the forefront in the child welfare industry. His vision and leadership for a revolution in residential care and counseling have proven effective. Robert has also built a strong following as the host of Straight Talk, a popular conservative radio program. His moving, inspiring testimony, together with his unique and timely perspective, has made Robert Day a sought after speaker for conferences, churches, civic audiences and beyond.

robertjdayauthor.org | patrickhenry.org

Straight Talk with Robert J. Day

... a radio broadcast ministry of
Patrick Henry Family Services

*Uplifting and encouraging messages on many of the most
challenging issues facing children and families today.*

**Hear Robert J. Day daily
at 7:20 am and 4:20 pm
on Spirit FM.**

Not in Virginia? ... you can enjoy all
Straight Talks in both written and audio formats
on straighttalkwithrobertday.org.

... challenging the way we think and live!

AGAINST
THE
TIDE

FORGIVE ME IF I AM EXAGGERATING but it seems to me that we've become a society that would rather worship celebrities than honor heroes. In our media mad mentally, personality now trumps character. I guess that's what happens when a nation of doers becomes a nation of spectators.

We have become a culture that now esteems popularity over truth, where everyone has followers and their worth is measured by the number of likes, hits, and shares they can get, not by their contribution or service to the country. Many have become more motivated by the fear of hurt and rejection than by the search for truth and honor.

Just how do we turn this around? Well, we can decide today we will no longer be a part of the cultural narcissism. We can resolve to swim against the tide. No one has to follow, or like, or share in our counter-cultural protest. Cultures change one person at a time. Let the change we seek start with us.

In Need of a Speaker for Your Next Event?

Now you can have *Robert J. Day* as keynote speaker for your next conference, meeting or other event.

Check out the full team of dynamic speakers and presenters from the Patrick Henry Family Services Speakers Bureau at patrickhenry.org or by calling 434.239.6891